CHARLES ROSS

The Wars of the Roses

A CONCISE HISTORY

with 126 illustrations

THAMES AND HUDSON

ACKNOWLEDGMENTS

I am grateful to Mrs Valerie Jane Coles and Mr Geoffrey Wheeler for their invaluable assistance in the selection of illustrations for this book. My colleagues in the University of Bristol, Mr P. V. McGrath, Mr J. W. Sherborne and Mr J. V. Scattergood, have advised me, to my considerable benefit, on a number of points, as has Dr R. A. Griffiths of the University College of Swansea. Finally, I am deeply indebted to my wife, Anne, for her constant advice and encouragement, and not least for saving me from many errors in the genealogical thickets which inevitably confront any student of the Wars of the Roses.

Printed and bound in Singapore by C.S. Graphics

CONTENTS

Chapter One

INTRODUCTION
THE WARS OF THE ROSES IN HISTORICAL TRADITION

> What misery, what murder and what execrable plagues this famous region hath suffered by the division and dissension of the renowned houses of Lancaster and York, my wit cannot comprehend nor my tongue declare, neither yet my pen fully set forth. For what noble man liveth at this day, or what gentleman of any ancient stock or progeny . . . whose lineage hath not been infested and plagued with this unnatural division.

In these words the Tudor historian and publicist, Edward Hall, writing in 1548, set forth the peculiar horror which sixteenth-century Englishmen felt for civil strife. This revulsion sprang largely from the fears and perils of their own time: repeated rebellions, dynastic uncertainties, religious divisions and the stresses imposed by economic and social changes. But it was also encouraged by generations of official Tudor apologists, anxious to impress upon their fellow-countrymen how the establishment of the Tudor dynasty had saved England from the vicious and damaging civil conflict which had wracked the country during the quarrels between the Houses of Lancaster and York. They tended to see the whole of fifteenth-century English history as a drama directed by God. The first Lancastrian king, Henry IV, had sinned by his unrighteousness in deposing Richard II. Eventually his sins were visited on the third generation of his family in the person of Henry VI, who was brought down, in a welter of blood, by the agents of divine retribution, the House of York. The Yorkists were themselves sinful, and reached a climax of wickedness in Richard III. Divine justice intervened again, and this time the saviour of England was Henry VII, whose marriage to Princess Elizabeth of York united the warring Houses, and made possible the triumphant reign of their son, Henry VIII.

This idea was largely popularized, but not invented, by one of the earliest and most influential of the Tudor apologists, the Italian humanist, Polydore Vergil, who acted as a sort of official historian to Henry VII and Henry VIII. (He did not invent it because it was already a theme of Yorkist propaganda, although naturally without

Opposite: the capture of Richard II, deposed by Henry of Bolingbroke, who began the line of Lancastrian kings as Henry IV, in 1399.

the unforeseen Tudor epilogue; and much later it was to be used again, in a further historical extension for the benefit of the Stuart dynasty, by Sir Walter Raleigh in his *History of the World*.) From Polydore the idea of divine retribution reached down to Shakespeare, in whom, however, it was often in dire conflict with notions of fate, fortune, the limited influence of free will and the malign or benignant influence of the stars.

Shakespeare, the great Duke of Marlborough once remarked, was the only English history book he had ever read, and the playwright's influence remains enormous. Yet he was far from being the only Tudor Englishman to write at length on the horrors of civil war, a theme springing from the deep-felt need for order and unity. The same subject was taken up by other dramatists, by historians (often thinly disguised as propagandists), by poets, and by political theorists such as Sir Thomas More, whose *History of King Richard III* is very much a treatise on tyranny. All of them shared the deep Renaissance belief that history, the queen of sciences, existed above all (as Dr Johnson put it) 'to point a moral and adorn a tale'. It was a quarry of examples. Lessons might and should be learnt, guidelines for future generations deduced from past experience. The Tudors' search for the inescapable truths of history led them naturally to their own immediate English past, to the fifteenth century. They studied with anxious concern 'the unquiet time of Henry IV', 'the troublous season of Henry VI' and 'the tragical doings of Richard III',

Head of Richard III: wood-carving on a misericord, Christchurch, Hampshire.

to quote some of the chapter-headings of Edward Hall's successful and influential work *The Union of the two Noble and Illustre families of Lancastre and Yorke.*

All this explains the remarkably large volume of writing, in whatever genre, about the fifteenth century, and especially about the Wars of the Roses, which found its way into print in Tudor England. In Shakespeare, for example, it accounts for no less than eight of the thirty-seven plays in the accepted canon. But the pre-occupations, prejudices and often deliberately propagandist purpose of these writings also served to give the Tudor version of fifteenth-century history a peculiarly high and bloody colour. The horrors of the civil war were artificially heightened to add point to the writer's own purpose.

The union – in propaganda at least – of Lancaster and York: an early sixteenth-century votive altarpiece in which Henry VII and Elizabeth of York, with their children, are shown in adoration of St George.

In Shakespeare's hands, civil war reached a high point of terror. With dramatic licence to avoid (except for passing mention) 'this weak piping time of peace', to telescope events so that the cruel highlights are illuminated, even to introduce avenging ghosts into the dreams of a remorseful king, the picture became much more terrifying. To see enacted, or even to read through, the three parts of Shakespeare's *Henry VI*, and his *Richard III*, is to be confronted, in rapid sequence, with a dreadful picture of carnage, battles, executions, murder, treachery, ambition and the shedding of innocent blood. Great playwright as he was, Shakespeare heightens the effect with contrasting touches of nobility, pathos, loyalty and affection, but none of this can stop the march of historical inevitability. Both weak and strong are struck down; the stage of history is littered with the corpses of innocent and guilty alike. Not until Henry of Richmond triumphs at Bosworth, as the prelude to his accession as Henry VII, can we pause at last and see a brighter future:

> O, now, let Richmond and Elizabeth,
> The true succeeders of each royal house . . .
> Enrich the time to come with smooth-faced peace,
> With smiling plenty, and fair prosperous days!
> Abate the edge of traitors, gracious Lord,
> That would reduce these bloody days again
> And make poor England weep in streams of blood! . . .
> Now civil wounds are stopped, peace lives again:
> That she may long live here, God say Amen!

This interpretation of the Wars of the Roses held the field for a remarkably long time. Even the great scholars of the nineteenth century, who did so much to establish history as an academic and reasonably unbiased discipline, did little to correct it. Their own dislike of bloody civil war and factional strife was reinforced by their belief that the Wars of the Roses checked the ordered advance of England towards the liberal parliamentary democracy which ruled the golden heyday of Imperial Victorian England. In one rather extreme example – J.C. Denton's *England in the Fifteenth Century*, published in 1888 – we find the old story of a series of bloody battles, which decimated the nobility and cost the lives of 100,000 men, while as many more died from want, exposure and disease. Commerce was destroyed, the towns ruined, the land lay waste for want of hands to till it. All in all, we are told,'Civilization and refinement had gone back and English life at the accession of Henry VII was far behind the England of the thirteenth century.'

The twentieth century has seen a sharp reaction against this gloomy and traditional view. With a fuller and more sympathetic understanding of late-medieval politics, modern scholars have attempted to expound the civil strife in terms which fifteenth-century people would have understood, to set forth the real and genuine political issues which produced the civil war, rather than to project backwards their own prejudices. The result has been to

The seated boar: hat-badge
of Richard III's retainers

produce a much less cynical picture of fifteenth-century political
society. The importance of the fighting, of the numbers of men
engaged, of the numbers of casualties – all these have been severely
played down. For most Englishmen, it is now argued, the war had
little relevance. The evils which afflicted fifteenth-century society
were already present before the fighting began. The civil wars did
little either to make them worse or to cure them. It changed nothing
and had few lasting effects. Above all, it is argued, the wars had
remarkably little impact on English civilization in general. The arts
of peace – commerce, education, religious life, writing, architecture,
painting – all went on as before. Is this modern reappraisal justified,
or have we now swung too far in the opposite direction? Were the
Wars of the Roses really so relatively unimportant in English
development as it is now fashionable to suppose?

Before turning to the central questions of this book, it may be as
well to attempt some justification for its title. For the very term
'The Wars of the Roses' – which has been such familiar coinage to
generations of historians, teachers and schoolchildren, to describe
the thirty-year period of civil war in England from 1455 to 1487 –
has recently been under fire. Some modern scholars have rather
grumpily objected to its use as being anachronistic and unhistorical.
They claim that the White Rose of York was only one among the
many badges used by the House of York, and that the last Yorkist
king, Richard III, was far better known by his personal badge of the
White Boar. Worse still, the so-called Red Rose of Lancaster was
not used at all by Henry VI, the chief Lancastrian protagonist in the

comfort Et Lyesse

pense

famm̄

Spayn̄

civil wars, although it became the principal badge of Henry Tudor after his accession to the throne as Henry VII in 1485. The earliest use of the phrase, at least in print, seems to have been by David Hume, in his *History of England*, published in 1762.

Yet the *idea*, if not the precise phrase, has a long and respectable ancestry. It was already common currency in the time of Shakespeare, who starts the civil war from the scene in the Temple gardens (*Henry VI*, I. II, sc. iv) where the rival leaders, John Beaufort, Duke of Somerset, Henry VI's principal minister, and Richard, Duke of York, who was later to claim Henry's throne, symbolically pluck the red and white roses and distribute them among their followers. It occurs again and again throughout Shakespeare's tetralogy on the Wars of the Roses, until in the closing scene of *Richard III*, the victorious Henry Tudor pronounces:

> And then, as we have ta'en the sacrament,
> We will unite the White Rose and the Red:
> Smile heaven upon this fair conjunction,
> That long have frowned upon their enmity!

Obviously the Red Rose is here taken as the badge of Lancaster, not merely of Tudor. But the same idea was already well established some eighty years before Shakespeare wrote. Henry VII was at pains, in his royal pageantry and propaganda, to stress the fact that he was

Opposite: the standard of Henry VII, with Tudor badges and devices, including the thorn-bush (*top left*), double roses and rose on sunburst (*centre*) and the portcullis of the Beaufort family.

The fifteenth-century manuscript *Cultivement des Terres*, produced for Edward IV, contains the white rose in the border. This rose was certainly the best-known Yorkist badge, as we might further judge from the border of the *Chemin de Vaillance* (*opposite*), also produced for Edward.

the true heir to the House of Lancaster, for which the Red Rose stood symbol, and that his marriage had united the rival families. The idea quickly took hold. The court poet, Stephen Hawes, a member of Henry VII's household and responsible for his 'ballet' performances, could say in an address to the newly crowned Henry VIII:

> Two tytles in one thou dydest well unyfye
> Whan the red rose toke the white in maryage

Similarly, the poet laureate, John Skelton, himself tutor to Henry VIII, expressed the same idea in a poem written after his pupil's coronation in 1509:

The rose both white and rede
In one rose now dothe growe.

Perhaps the earliest reference to the symbol of the opposing roses comes in the 'Croyland Chronicle', written, probably, by Bishop John Russell of Lincoln, Chancellor of England under Richard III, and completed by April 1486, within nine months of the Battle of Bosworth. In the midst of his narrative the author includes a few lines of verse in which Richard III is represented as paying the penalty on the battlefield of Bosworth for the murder of the princes in the Tower (see p. 95) – this is also the first direct *English* reference to his guilt. They end:

the Boar's [Richard III's] tusks quailed
And, to avenge the White, the Red Rose bloomed.

Here, perhaps, the author had in mind the Red Rose of Tudor, but at almost the same time as he was writing, the city of York was preparing to receive King Henry VII on his first official progress. One of the pageant-devices used was the intertwined two-coloured rose, and this was the precursor of thousands of such references, in architecture, art, music and literature, to symbolize the union of Lancaster and York. Before 1485, it is true, it is much harder to find references to the idea of opposing roses, although the White Rose of York was that family's most famous badge, and is widely scattered in manuscripts, in heraldry and in political verse, where Edward IV himself is regularly called (after his place of birth) 'The Rose of Rouen'. Perhaps the idea was the product of clever Tudor propaganda, but after almost five hundred years of regular use, it is surely pedantic now to reject it, particularly when it was already accepted and used by the very generation which had lived through the wars themselves. Unrepentedly, therefore, I make it the title of this book.

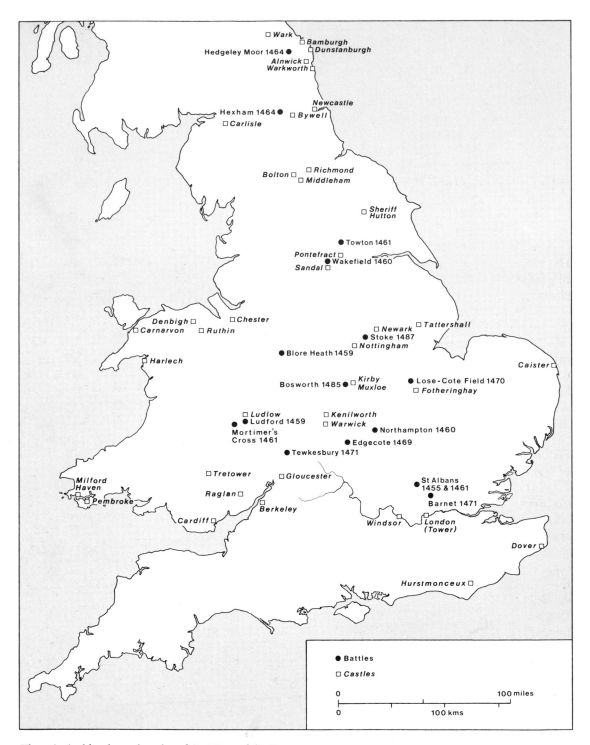

The principal battles and castles of the Wars of the Roses.

Chapter Two

THE ORIGINS OF THE CIVIL WAR

Henry V was probably the most able king ever to occupy the throne of England. Yet, for all his brilliant achievements both at home and abroad, his legacy to his country was a gloomy one. When he died at Vincennes in August 1422, still in his thirty-fifth year, the heir to the thrones of England and France was his infant son, Henry VI, who was less than nine months old, and the country faced the longest minority in its history. The ambitious war of conquest in France which Henry V had begun in 1415 was far from complete and the larger part of France remained outside his control. The French wars had already saddled the English crown with a heavy burden of debt which increased steadily under the crippling strain of another twenty-two years of campaigning; and Henry's preoccupation with France effectively prevented him from tackling the urgent problems of lawlessness and disorder which afflicted his realm of England.

All these difficulties were to contribute, albeit indirectly, to the outbreak of civil war thirty-three years later. A royal minority was always a fertile breeding-time for factional dispute, and the absence of an effective king inevitably reduced the royal control over the already powerful aristocracy, many of whose members were involved in competition for the profits of political power. In France the slow tide of English conquest rolled on under the able direction of Henry V's elder surviving brother, John, Duke of Bedford, until checked at Orleans in 1429 by the appearance of Joan of Arc and the beginnings of French recovery. In 1435 English fortunes received a further blow with the death of Bedford himself and the defection of England's principal ally, the Duke of Burgundy. Thereafter English arms were thrown sharply on the defensive, and the conquest of France ceased to be a realistic objective. The question of whether to continue the war or to make peace with France now became a serious issue in English domestic politics, with the chief protagonists for power, the king's great-uncle, Henry Beaufort, Cardinal Bishop of Winchester, and his uncle, the popular but irresponsible Humphrey, Duke of Gloucester, taking opposite

The birth of Henry VI (*above*), only nine months before the death of his father, Henry V, was soon followed by a number of years of rule by aristocratic council. Richard Beauchamp, Earl of Warwick (d. 1439), who bears the infant king on his left arm (*above right*), was entrusted with Henry's upbringing.

sides. The cost of many years of continued warfare mounted steadily, especially since Parliament was becoming increasingly reluctant to vote taxes for an unsuccessful war. In England itself a high level of disorder, much of it produced by powerful offenders against whom it was difficult to obtain redress at law, continued unchecked, and feuds and quarrels among a land-hungry nobility increased in number and violence.

Yet none of these problems was insuperable when Henry VI, at the unusually early age of sixteen, declared his minority at an end in November 1437, and claimed to rule in his own name. The aristocratic council which had governed England since 1422 had shown a high degree of political responsibility. With help from John, Duke of Bedford, it had successfully contained the bitter rivalries of Beaufort and Gloucester, and several disputes between leading English magnates. By intelligent and realistic diplomacy the English might still have obtained a respectable peace-settlement with France and retained the hard core of Henry V's French conquests. Prudent management could have done much to restore a degree of financial solvency, especially if a peace treaty or a prolonged period of truce had removed the heavy drain of money resulting from the war. As Henry V had shown, an active and forceful king could quell quarrels among his magnates, and the English crown had reserves

of patronage to satisfy all those who sought royal favour, if properly used. Henry VI's royal inheritance, if somewhat tarnished, was still largely intact in 1437. Had he been half the man his father was, the disasters which followed his assumption of power might readily have been avoided.

For a variety of reasons the personality of the reigning king was a decisive element in medieval English politics. Although over some three hundred years an elaborate and reasonably efficient bureaucracy had been developed, England remained very much a monarchy. The higher direction of policy, especially foreign affairs, and much of the day-to-day administration of government, still required the personal participation of the king. In particular – and this was a vital area where the management of his great men was concerned – it was the king's business to make intelligent use of his royal patronage. Quite apart from a complete control of all the higher offices in the church and in the legal profession, and of all promotions to the nobility, he had at his disposal a series of rewards and appointments. These ranged from great military or political commands, like the offices of Captain of Calais, Chief Justices of North and South Wales, and Wardens of the Marches towards Scotland, down to the constableships of royal castles and stewardships of royal manors, or profitable sinecures like the office of Surveyor of the King's Mines

The coronation of Henry VI as King of France at Paris in 1430 was not the prelude to final English victory, despite the capture of Joan of Arc (*above left*, before Paris) the following year. The Duke of Burgundy, Philip the Good, seen (*above*) with his young son, the future Charles the Bold, was reconciled with the French king in 1435.

or Master of the Royal Mint. Moreover, the king disposed of large numbers of wardships or custodies of baronial and gentry estates which came into his hands during the minority of their heirs, together with the marriages of those heirs, both male and female; and these were all marketable commodities, for which the landowning classes, anxious to secure or improve the fortunes of their family dynasties, eagerly competed. In addition, the royal reservoir of patronage had been vastly increased in 1399 when the accession of Henry IV brought the Duchy of Lancaster to the crown. This was the greatest private estate of the entire medieval period, inherited by Henry from his father, John of Gaunt. The Duchy was kept separate from the ordinary royal land-administration, and hundreds of profitable offices, pensions and annuities which could be charged upon its revenues were entirely at the personal disposal of the reigning king: they had been successfully used by Henry IV and Henry V to win the loyalty and service of a large and powerful royal affinity. In an England which possessed neither standing army nor police force, the king was inevitably dependent upon the military resources, local influence and goodwill of the nobility and the richer gentry to maintain law and order and to carry on routine government in the shires; but he did have ample resources of patronage with which to attract their co-operation.

Unfortunately, Henry VI was far from being the right man to cope effectively with the admittedly serious problems which faced an English ruler in 1437. Today, our view of his character and abilities is seriously obscured both by the bias of chroniclers writing during the Yorkist period and by the deliberate propaganda-image projected by Tudor authors, beginning with Polydore Vergil, and ultimately enshrined by Shakespeare himself, with overweening authority, in English folk-psychology. The former presented him as essentially a simpleton, easily led and dominated by 'covetous counsel'; the latter as a guileless saint. Both images are much in keeping with the vacant features of the stock portraits of Henry, all of them executed after 1485. Unfortunately, comments on Henry's character by people writing before the Yorkist usurpation of 1461 are few and meagre, but they lend some support to the notion that he was indeed a man of limited mental capacity who was too much influenced by those around him. Probably Abbot Whetehamstede of St Albans came nearest the mark when he praised Henry as a simple and upright man who could not resist those who urged him to unwise decisions and wasteful prodigality.

We know that he was a peace-loving man, who was notably more merciful on occasions than most of his contemporaries, and who did his limited best to heal the feuds among his great men. He was a

Following his coronation as King of France (*opposite*), Henry VI appointed John Talbot, Earl of Shrewsbury, as Constable of the country (*below*).

Henry VI: from Ricart's *Mayor's Calendar of Bristol, c.* 1480.

The more familiar stock portrait of Henry VI, produced in large numbers for the picture-galleries of country houses.

Henry VI's foundation charter for King's College, Cambridge: the miniature depicts the opening of Parliament, with the Lords, and below them the Commons, kneeling before the king.

faithful husband and a loving father; he was deeply religious and closely interested in education – his foundations of Eton College and King's College, Cambridge, are his most positive personal achievements; but, at least according to his confessor, he became increasingly preoccupied with these interests at the expense of the less pleasing business of governing the realm. Some modern historians have challenged this long-accepted characterization of the king, and have argued that he was not such a simpleton as had been supposed, and, indeed, that at least in the early years it was his actions rather than his inaction which were responsible for many of the disasters. One recent writer has argued persuasively that between 1437 and 1448 he intervened frequently, and with disastrous results, in the conduct of foreign policy, and, moreover, seriously weakened the financial position and political reputation of the crown by an unprecedentedly lavish distribution of titles, offices, lands and pensions to the friends who surrounded him in 1437 and later. The result was to create an entrenched court party which had a vested interest in keeping control of the king's person and excluding all its rivals from access to him. It is doubtful, however, whether this activity persisted into the 1450s, when he seems to become for most purposes a political cipher, more and more under the control of his counsellors and of his French wife, the high-spirited, auto-cratic and ruthless Margaret of Anjou. In 1453 he suffered a severe nervous breakdown, perhaps some legacy of the mental instability

Above: detail from a tapestry produced at the time of Henry VI's betrothal to Margaret of Anjou, showing Margaret's cipher on the horses' trappings, with (*left*) what is said to be the marriage ceremony itself.

of his maternal grandfather, the Valois king, Charles VI of France, who had been a raving lunatic for years on end. What is certain is that Henry was notably lacking in the qualities of force of character and intelligence necessary to command the respect and fear of his great men, and that he soon came to be regarded, both by friends and critics, as excessively malleable to the wishes of whoever happened to have control of him at any particular time.

Within a few years of Henry's coming-of-age, the government's difficulties had become acute. Major diplomatic miscalculations led to the reopening of the war with France, at a time when England was totally unprepared for large-scale conflict; the result was the loss within the space of a few months of all Henry V's conquests in northern France. At home the king's debts mounted spectacularly, and this was due less to the costs of the French campaigns than to Henry VI's excessive generosity. Estimated at £164,000 in 1433 in a budget statement, these debts stood at £372,000 in 1450, at a time when the regular annual income of the crown was probably less than £33,000. Complaints mounted against the greed, corruption and partiality of Henry's leading ministers, and the oppression, gangsterism and perversion of the law in the shires by those who had the backing of powerful men at Westminster. In March 1450 growing discontent with the regime exploded with the impeachment by the Commons in Parliament of Henry's principal minister, William de la Pole, Duke of Suffolk, and, even more alarming, with the outbreak in May of a well-supported popular rebellion in the south-east, generally known as the Rebellion of Jack Cade. Unlike the Peasants' Revolt of 1381 this was not motivated primarily by economic and social grievances; the main complaints of the rebels were essentially political, and constituted a massive indictment of the regime, in particular of the ministers in whom Henry continued to trust. As the rebels themselves expressed it:

> Also the law serves for nought else in these days but to do wrong, for nothing is sped almost but false matters by colour of the law for bribery, dread, and favour. . . . Also we say our sovereign lord may understand that his false council has lost his law, his merchandise is lost, his common people is lost, the sea is lost, France is lost, the king himself is so beset that he may not pay for his meat and drink, and he owes more than ever any King of England ought, for daily his traitors about him, when any thing should come to him by his laws, at once ask it from him.

Opposite: pictorial genealogy, showing the descent of Henry VI (*bottom centre*) from St Louis of France (*top*) through the kings of France on the left and the kings of England on the right. The supporters are the royal dukes, Humphrey of Gloucester and Richard of York.

The government survived both the fall of Suffolk and the challenge of Cade's Rebellion only to be confronted later in the year with another and ultimately more dangerous assault upon its political prestige. This was the reappearance in England of Duke Richard of York, Henry VI's Lieutenant in Ireland, who now returned in order to make capital out of the voluminous discontents of the previous months. Duke Richard was the most prominent and powerful of the great magnates alive in 1450 who could claim descent from King

Edward III. On his father's side he was descended from Edmund of Langley, 1st Duke of York and fourth son of Edward III (John of Gaunt, progenitor of the House of Lancaster, being the third son); but through his mother, Anne Mortimer, he was descended from Lionel of Clarence, Edward's second son. If a claim to the throne through a female were allowed – though neither precedent nor ruling existed on this point – his title was superior to that of Henry VI himself. This issue, however, was not raised immediately, although in 1451 one of York's supporters in Parliament, Thomas Young, MP for Bristol, put forward a petition that York should at least be recognized as heir apparent to the still childless Henry VI, a claim which promptly landed Young in the Tower of London.

York's reasons for intervention in 1450 were at once personal and concerned with the public interest. In spite of his close blood-relationship with the king, he had been largely excluded from the royal councils. As Henry's principal commander in France, he had seen himself slyly superseded by his rival, Edmund Beaufort, Duke of Somerset, who was himself a potential heir to Henry VI. Owed vast sums by an impecunious government for his services in France, he had been constantly refused payment while Somerset got first claim on the available funds; finally he had been shuffled off to a virtual exile as King's Lieutenant in Ireland. But he was also the political heir of Duke Humphrey of Gloucester, the advocate of Henry V's aggressive policy in France, whose death in 1447 looked as if it may have been murder by government partisans who found his criticisms intolerable. York was particularly incensed by the loss of France and the abandonment of Henry V's French conquests; his later record suggests that York had some genuine and unselfish concern for the restoration of good government. In 1450 his plan was to secure the backing of the Commons in Parliament, to remove Somerset and at least some of the more obnoxious members of the royal household, and to push through an Act of Resumption which would cancel all the lavish grants to royal favourites made in the past few years. In this scheme he achieved only temporary success, for as soon as Parliament was dissolved, Henry felt free to ignore its demands.

York had thus failed to impose himself upon the king by 'constitutional' means, and in 1452 he resorted to force. Duke Richard seems to have been a man of conservative temperament, a somewhat austere, remote and unsympathetic figure, with little capacity or inclination to seek and win support from his fellow-noblemen or from the wider public. He was also impulsive and inclined to act without consultation; and his attempt at an armed *coup d'état* in 1452 was the first of a series of political miscalculations. He singularly failed to appreciate that in the eyes of the nobility there was a vast difference between his presenting himself as a champion of reform and retrenchment by peaceful methods, and his taking up arms against his anointed king. The result was humiliating failure, for

the only man of consequence who supported him was the turbulent and self-interested Earl of Devon. Confronted by a royal army, which included most of his fellow-magnates, York had no choice but to grovel before the king and retire in disgrace to his castle of Ludlow in the Marches of Wales. He was not to re-emerge until April 1454 when he was appointed Protector of England during Henry's prolonged illness.

By May 1455, however, the situation had radically changed in York's favour. The main reason was a swing in political allegiance by the most powerful and certainly the most numerous family group in fifteenth-century England. The fortunes of the northern family of Nevill were founded by Ralph Nevill, 1st Earl of Westmorland (d. 1425), who had been much favoured by Richard II as a counterpart to the Percies, Earls of Northumberland, and whose

The great estates of Richard Beauchamp, Earl of Warwick – seen here being invested with the Order of the Garter by Henry IV – descended to Warwick the Kingmaker, and later to the Dukes of Clarence and Gloucester, all of whom played a key role in the Wars.

second marriage to Joan Beaufort, daughter of John of Gaunt, Duke of Lancaster, brought him into close association with the royal House of Lancaster. The interests of their twelve children were promoted with unparalleled lack of scruple and with great success. The eldest son of the marriage, Richard Nevill, was married to a wealthy heiress, Alice Montagu, through whom he acquired the title and estates of the earldom of Salisbury. Three of his brothers married the heiresses of the baronial families of Fauconberg, Latimer and Abergavenny (even though one of these ladies was a declared lunatic), a fourth became Bishop of Durham, and their sisters married into the greatest families of England. One of them, Cecily Nevill, became wife to Richard of York himself. In the next generation, Salisbury's eldest son, also named Richard, became an even greater landowner through marriage to the ultimate heiress of the wealthiest of the English earls, Richard Beauchamp, Earl of Warwick (d. 1439).

Until 1452 their Beaufort ties and profitable court connections had kept the Nevill group closely associated with the government, but for some years previously there had been growing tension in the north of England between the Nevills and the Percies, as the former steadily increased their influence in the north-west, traditionally a region of Percy dominance. In 1453–54 this hostility exploded into private war which threw much of the north, especially Yorkshire, into turmoil, and there were pitched battles (if on a small scale) at Heworth near York and at Stamford Bridge not far away. At the same time the young Nevill, Earl of Warwick, had come into conflict with the Duke of Somerset on his own account. Warwick, on whom later generations were to bestow the sobriquet of 'the Kingmaker', had energy, dash and courage. A skilful propagandist, he had great success in rousing the common people to his cause and was well known for his open-handed generosity. Yet he was also self-interested and arrogant, and, like the rest of the Nevill family, acquisitive and unscrupulous to a degree; he was to prove himself unusually ruthless in his treatment of defeated enemies. When he blatantly defied the laws of inheritance, even against his own kinsman of Abergavenny, and sought to hold the entire lordship of Glamorgan by force against the Duke of Somerset, to whom the king had granted its keeping, he too joined the rest of the Nevill group in overt support of York. Meanwhile, Northumberland and his friends, who now included the violent and stupid Henry Holland, Duke of Exeter (Henry VI's nearest male relative), aligned themselves with the court faction.

When York became Protector of England during Henry VI's illness, he tried as far as possible to rule through a broad-based administration, and to draw the nobility behind him in a governing council reminiscent of the days of Henry VI's minority. Inevitably, however, when he intervened in private wars in a laudable attempt to restore order, he emerged as a partisan, backing his Nevill friends

Opposite: Ralph Nevill, 1st Earl of Westmorland, with the twelve children of his second marriage to Joan Beaufort, daughter of John of Gaunt. Among the sons, Richard Nevill, Earl of Salisbury, and William, Lord Fauconberg, were important supporters of the House of York.

in the north; and, in a similar situation in the west country, he backed Lord Bonville against his erstwhile friend, the Earl of Devon, who had switched sides since 1452. His official appointments also had their partisan colour: Salisbury became Chancellor of England in April 1454, and York himself took over the important captaincy of Calais from the Duke of Somerset, now temporarily in prison.

Finally, these years saw the emergence of Queen Margaret of Anjou as York's most bitter and uncompromising opponent. Henry's breakdown in health coincided with the birth in October 1453 of their only child, Edward, Prince of Wales: and Henry's uncertain condition not unnaturally inspired in the queen fears for the secure succession of her son. Moreover, she was balked of her claim to be regent during her husband's illness by the lords' preference for the Duke of York as Protector. Her response was to ally herself with the extremist elements at court, many of them York's personal enemies, and the destruction of York, as a potential threat to the Lancastrian succession, became her principal aim. She may well have been behind the politically provocative acts which followed hard on the heels of Henry's recovery of health and the formal ending of the Protectorate in February 1455.

This was the situation which produced the first battle of the civil war proper. The Yorkist leaders found themselves politically once more in the cold and threatened by the renewed favours shown to their enemies, especially Somerset and Exeter. Their alarm was further increased when they were summoned to appear before a great council at Leicester, which was probably intended to force them into an oath of submission similar to that exacted from York after the Dartford affair. Their reply was to arm. On 22 May 1455, after negotiations between the parties had collapsed, they clashed with a hastily assembled royalist force at St Albans. The essentially factious nature of the strife is clearly revealed by the course of the battle itself, for as soon as Somerset, Northumberland and his friend, Lord Clifford, had been killed, the fighting ceased. York and the Nevills had triumphed over their personal enemies: their prize was to take possession of the person of Henry VI (who had been slightly wounded in the fighting) and establish a short-lived Yorkist administration – the so-called Second Protectorate of York – based upon this control of the king.

For four years after the 1st Battle of St Albans an uneasy peace reigned. What prevented the renewal of armed conflict was partly the peace-making efforts of the king himself, backed by some of the bishops and by a magnate almost as great as York himself in terms of wealth and influence, Humphrey Stafford, 1st Duke of Buckingham. Even more important was the reluctance of the nobility as a whole to become involved in civil war, and their continued loyalty to the person of King Henry. For, whatever the manifest defects of his administration, the king was regarded as a man set

Here shewes howe the said dame Anne countesse of warwyk doughter to the forsaid
Erle Richard hole suster & heire to hem duc of warwyk, was maryed to
Richard nevill sone & heire to Richard nevill the ... and
doughter & heire to ...
And the said Anne hadde
ij doughters / the first was
first wedded to prince
and secondly she was ...
after kyng of England
named Isabell / ware wedded
... by this portrature

... erle of Salisbury
by her forsaid husband
called Anne quene of England
Edward sone to kyng hen...
wedded to Richard duc of Glou...
and her second doughter
to George duc of Clarence
is more pleinly shewed

Richard nevill son to Richard Erle of Salisbury wedded Anne Countesse of warwyk

Anne Countesse of warwyk suster & heire to hem duc of warwyk

Prince Edward son to kyng hen the first husbond of Anne

Anne doughter to the forsaid Richard and first wiff to prince & last to kyng Richard

Kyng Richard the Second husbond to this Anne

George duc of Clar

Isabel duches of Clarence seconde doughter to the said Erle Anne

Edward Plantagenet son to kyng Richard

Edward Plantagenet son to George duc of Clarence

Margaret suster to the said Edward

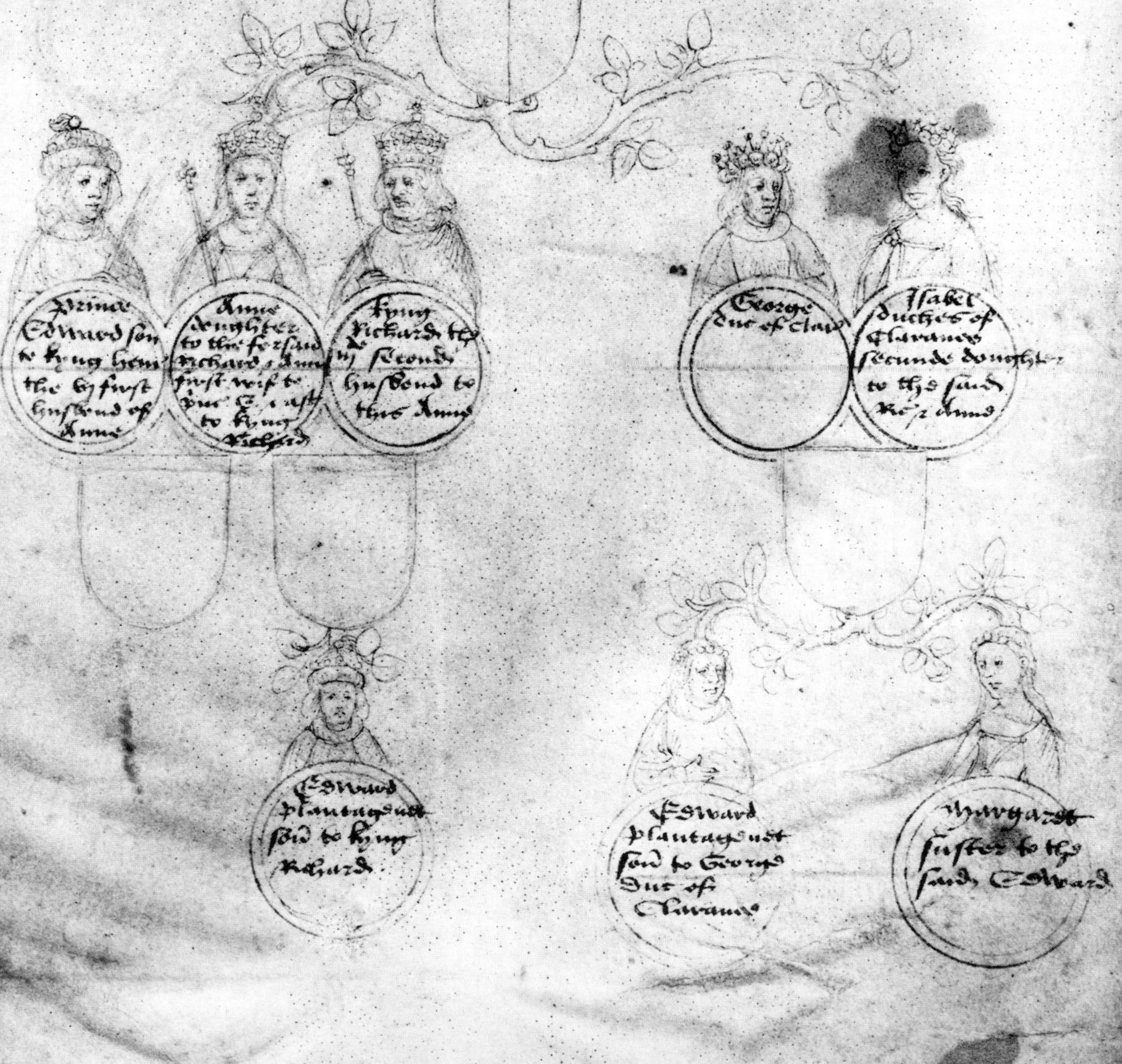

Henry VI's coronation as King of England in 1429. Loyalty to the person of the anointed king was an important factor in the early stages of the Wars of the Roses.

apart from other men by the solemn rites of his coronation: in particular, the ceremony of unction (his anointing with holy oil) made him a semi-divine being. Moreover, all the lords, including York and his friends, had repeatedly pledged solemn oaths of loyalty to the person of King Henry, which were not lightly to be broken even in that rather cynical age. These stubborn sentiments of devotion were very much a factor to be reckoned with at the beginning of the civil war (although later eroded by political violence); and for this reason any attempt to kill the king, or even to depose him by peaceful methods, would have been a grave miscalculation, as Duke Richard discovered to his cost in 1460. Nor were the great majority of barons willing to take up arms against the king, whatever the real or imagined grievances of York and his supporters. It was

above all the influence of the queen that brought about the resumption of civil war in the autumn of 1459, for her dominance over her husband seems to have increased in these years. In 1460 Pope Pius II believed (although his information came from a biased source) that Henry VI was 'a man more timorous than a woman, utterly devoid of wit or spirit, who left everything in his wife's hands'.

Under Margaret's influence the court largely withdrew from London and took up residence in the Midlands in places such as Kenilworth, Coventry and Chester, where the resources of the Duchy of Lancaster and the Prince of Wales's earldom of Chester could be mobilized to build up support for the dynasty: a hostile Yorkist chronicler tells us that 'she allied unto her all the knights and squires of Cheshire for to have their benevolence, and held open

The image of Henry VI as a brave warrior – here in a manuscript produced for Margaret of Anjou – made a strange contrast with his true personality. His total lack of military prowess was a great weakness for the Lancastrian cause.

Margaret of Anjou, presented with a book, *c.* 1445.

household among them; and made her son called the Prince give a livery of Swans to all the gentlemen of the country, and to many others throughout the land.' In general, he continued, 'the queen with such as were of her affinity [following] ruled the realm as her liked, gathering riches innumerable' and 'the realm was out of all good governance'. Moreover, Margaret associated herself with outright partisans, mostly declared enemies of the Duke of York. Among them were the Earls of Shrewsbury and Wiltshire, who succeeded each other as Treasurers of England between 1456 and 1460, and the sons of the noblemen who had been killed at St Albans. The young men who now succeeded as Duke of Somerset, Earl of Northumberland and Lord Clifford had obvious reasons for disliking the men who had caused their fathers' deaths. The king's half-brothers, Jasper Tudor, Earl of Pembroke, and Edmund Tudor, Earl of Richmond, were also working to increase royal influence and weaken that of Duke Richard in Wales and the Marches.

In this atmosphere of suspicion King Henry's efforts to heal the feuds and to allot compensation in the Nevill–Percy dispute and for

The white swan: livery badge of Margaret of Anjou, found near the battlefield of St Albans. Made in gold and white enamel, it was worn by a person of rank.

the St Albans' affair proved little more than a hollow sham, and behind the façade of a public reconciliation both parties were arming themselves. The so-called Loveday of 24 March 1458, when the rival factions marched arm-in-arm to St Paul's Cathedral, was conducted against the threatening backcloth of thousands of armed retainers quartered near by. What brought about the final rupture was Margaret's decision to crush her opponents by force. A great council was summoned to meet at Coventry on 24 June 1459, to which York and his friends were conspicuously not invited. Faced with indictments from this council, the Yorkist leaders planned to confront it in such force as to gain a hearing from the king, and arranged to meet at Ludlow to concert their course of action. The queen's party endeavoured to forestall this hostile concentration, and on 23 September 1459 the Earl of Salisbury, marching down from the north, clashed with a royalist army at Blore Heath in Shropshire. The battle was indecisive and he moved on to Ludlow. Confronted by a royal army led by the king in person, and seduced by the offer of a pardon, most of the Yorkist rank-and-file deserted at the 'Rout of Ludford' (12–13 October) and their leaders had no choice but to flee the realm. Duke Richard escaped to Ireland, where he had already won much support by offering the Anglo-Irish virtual independence of Westminster; Salisbury, Warwick, Fauconberg and York's eldest son, the young Edward, Earl of March, took ship for Calais, where Warwick had now been Captain for four years, and had defiantly retained his position despite government attempts to dislodge him. In November 1459, a packed Parliament met at Coventry and attainted the Yorkists; that is, they were declared rebels and all their lives, lands and goods were now forfeit to the crown. Thereafter they could return only by force. The issue was fairly joined.

This necessarily brief review of the events of Henry VI's majority rule shows that an adequate explanation of the outbreak of civil war may be found in personal and political factors, especially those stemming from the weakness of the king and the impossibility of finding a political, non-violent solution to the problems which this

Battle-scene from a manuscript (*c.* 1445) presented to Margaret of Anjou by the Earl of Shrewsbury.

involved. Some modern historians, however, have sought to find alternative or contributory explanations, often related to the deeper economic and social changes of the period. It has been argued, for example, that the economic recession of the mid-fifteenth century made the competition for political profits more acute and pressing. This recession particularly affected the landowning class, through falling rents and rising labour costs, and magnates with estates in Wales suffered especially, as the Welsh tenantry successfully resisted the seignorial claims of their English overlords. Yet it would be hard to establish that poverty proved a spur to political gangsterism, especially as most of the protagonists in the fighting – York, Warwick, Somerset and Buckingham – were all richer men than their fathers, through marriage, inheritance and the fruits of royal favour. It was the government's failure to pay its debts which may have influenced a man like York to challenge the administration; in contrast, Buckingham, whose Welsh revenues, like York's, were severely affected, remained loyal to the crown.

Equally, we can be suspicious of the linked argument that there was a causal connection between the ending of the Hundred Years War in 1453 and the eruption of civil strife very soon after. The magnates, it is said, were now deprived of the profits of war which had offset their falling rents, and instead plunged into domestic politics to redress their fortunes, while the return of thousands of disbanded soldiers provided would-be contenders for power with willing warriors. In fact, few of the higher nobility had been directly engaged in the later stages of the fighting in France; and, in an increasingly defensive war, the profits from plunder and ransom were not what they had been: only too often the government could not, or would not, pay its commanders their due wages. Nor was the rank-and-file of the armies in France a large body of men, for the English military establishment had been allowed to decay, and the addition of at most some 5,000 unemployed soldiers made little difference to a society where every man carried arms, where resort to violent self-help was all too frequent, and where a high level of lawlessness and disorder was tolerated as a fact of life. No nobleman needed to rely on returned soldiers to raise a force of armed men: he needed to look no further than his own household and tenantry to find men able and willing to follow him in warlike array.

For similar reasons, the argument that civil war was an inevitable product of the growth of 'bastard feudalism' is unconvincing. This was the system which enabled a nobleman to enrol men in his service by contracts or indentures in return for a cash annuity. Hence the size of his following or affinity would depend only on the depth of his purse, and was not restricted, as in the earlier phase of 'classical feudalism', to his feudal vassals who were also his tenants. Yet 'bastard feudalism' had been in existence since the earlier part of the fourteenth century, and in any case represented no significant social change. It was (as Dr G. A. Holmes expressed it) 'merely the late medieval version of a more permanent feature of English

Knights in combat: from a military roll, *c.* 1443.

Alnwick: formidable stronghold of the Percy Earls of Northumberland. It was their local rivals, the Nevills, rather than the king, who broke their control over the north in the early stages of the Wars; and they were soon to win power again.

social organization: the grouping of servants and followers, household and retinue, noble and servile dependents, around the great estate, supported and attracted by its wealth and influence'.

We should perhaps take more seriously the idea that the Wars of the Roses were 'the outcome of an escalation of private feuds'. The reign of Henry VI undoubtedly saw a steady increase in local violence and a deterioration in men's ability to gain redress at law. Only too often legal processes could easily be diverted by bribery and intimidation, and this was especially true where powerful or well-connected offenders were concerned. The surviving letters of the Paston family in East Anglia (a particularly disturbed region) show clearly how the local gangsterism of men like Sir Thomas Tuddenham or John Heydon was condoned and protected by their patron, William de la Pole, Duke of Suffolk, and how difficult it was for their victims to find any redress against them unless they too had a powerful patron. In this sense there was a clear interconnection between local and national politics. Lesser men involved in private quarrels, or seeking to establish their claims to land, and finding themselves unable to obtain remedy through the due processes of the law, turned instead to a lord, often one who was at odds with their own rivals. They took his livery and supported his interests; but in return for their service, they expected him to 'maintain' them in their quarrels, by whatever lawful or unlawful means he could muster. These were the evils of 'livery and maintenance' about which contemporaries so frequently and bitterly complained. As the central government became at once weaker and more partisan, such groupings of mutual advantage and protection tended to move higher up the social scale. When even powerful noblemen found themselves threatened by their private enemies, they too looked to the central protagonists for power, York and Somerset, for aid and protection.

Local rivalries thus help to explain the eventual alignment of parties or factions in the national strife, as we have seen with the Percy-Nevill feud; and to some extent, at regional or provincial level, the civil war continued to be dominated by this strong underlying theme of private rivalry. For the north of England, the true meaning of the civil war in its first phase of Yorkist victory was the overthrow of the Percies, Earls of Northumberland, and the overwhelming triumph of their Nevill rivals; and in the second phase (1469–71) Edward IV's reinstatement of the Percies contributed to the downfall of the Nevills. Developments of this kind had a further consequence, for as a region fell under the control of a particular family through the collapse of its rivals, so the dependence of the central government on the victor's goodwill and co-operation was increased. As we shall see, this was to have a vital effect on the national struggle, especially in the reign of Richard III, whose fate was largely decided by the attitudes of the two surviving great families of the north, the Stanleys and the Percies. In this way, the Wars of the Roses led to an increase in the power of 'the overmighty subjects' by making them even more overmighty.

Raby Castle, Co. Durham: first seat of the Nevills, the prolific family whose actions played an important part in determining the outcome of many of the phases of the Wars.

Yet it would be a mistake to see this 'escalation of private feuds' as a prime cause of the civil war. It was the consequence of, and not the reason for, weakness at the centre of government, the direct result of rule by an ineffective king who nevertheless chose to support a regime which was seen to be corrupt, partial and self-seeking to a degree. Henry V had already demonstrated that, in K.B. McFarlane's words, 'only an undermighty ruler had anything to fear from an overmighty subject'; and the lesson was to be taught again by Edward IV in his later years and even more forcefully and successfully by Henry VII. In the end, one is left to conclude that the chief cause of the Wars of the Roses is simple enough. As McFarlane aptly phrased it, 'Henry VI's head was too small for his father's crown.'

Chapter Three

CIVIL WAR AND DYNASTIC REVOLUTION, 1460–87

The years from 1460 to 1487 form the first truly revolutionary period in English history. What distinguishes this phase of political strife from its predecessors is that opposition groups or factions now regularly made it their main objective not to supplant the king's ministers, but to overthrow the king himself and replace him with an alternative of their own choice; and they sought to impose themselves by force. The crown itself became the coveted prize of warring factions. The results were spectacular. Within twenty-five years the crown changed hands no less than six times. The chief victims of this phase of violent political conflict were the kings themselves and their immediate families. No less than three of the five kings involved – Henry VI, Edward V and Richard III – died violent deaths, and the families of Lancaster and York were exterminated in the direct male line.

YORK AND LANCASTER 1460–64

The dynastic issue was not clearly raised until the return of Duke Richard of York from Ireland in the autumn of 1460. Before then, however, the Yorkist cause had already enjoyed a dramatic change of fortune. While York remained in Ireland, the earls in Calais successfully beat off Lancastrian attempts to oust them, financing themselves and their men by a campaign of indiscriminate piracy in the Narrow Seas.

They prepared the ground for an invasion of England by an intensive propaganda campaign, one of the first of its kind in English history. For the time being their posture was the traditional tongue-in-cheek claim that the king, guiltless himself, had been misled by evil counsellors, who had oppressed the church, reduced the crown to poverty, over-taxed the Commons and, through their extortions and oppressions, banished 'all rightwiseness and justice' from the realm. In particular, they accused the Earls of Shrewsbury and

Wiltshire and others, 'our mortal and extreme enemies', of having excluded them from their rightful places beside the king, 'dreading the charge that would be laid upon them of the misery, destruction and wretchedness of the said realm, whereof they be causes, and not the king, which is himself as noble, as virtuous, as righteous, and blessed of disposition, as any prince earthly'. Manifestos and broadsheets of this kind were backed by popular ballads and verses which presented the Yorkist leaders as potential saviours of the realm, come to cleanse the garden of England of the noxious weeds which choked it (they shared with Shakespeare a fondness for horticultural metaphor):

> Richard duke of York, Job thy servant insigne,
> Whom Satan not ceaseth to set at care and disdain,
> But by Thee preserved he may not be slain . . .
> Edward earl of March, whose fame the earth shall spread,
> Richard earl of Salisbury named prudence,
> With that noble knight and flower of manhood,
> Richard earl of Warwick shield of our defence.

They even enlisted to their cause the ambitious and self-seeking papal legate, Francesco de Coppini (afterwards disgraced and imprisoned by the pope for his most unseemly partisanship), and Coppini accompanied them to give their enterprise a misleading cloak of clerical approval.

On 26 June 1460 the Yorkist earls landed at Sandwich. Their invasion enjoyed two immediate advantages. Firstly, Kent was still bitter from the bloody measures of repression taken after the collapse of Cade's Rebellion and resentful of the fact that nothing had been done to correct the abuses against which the rebels had campaigned. Secondly, the Lancastrian government had done little to win the loyalty of London. The trade of the capital had suffered from the general economic recession, and there was strong feeling against the favour shown to alien merchants by Henry VI's ministers. Many London merchants had invested heavily in the Yorkist control of Calais and a Yorkist administration seemed to be the only way to recover their loans. The court's removal to the Midlands had put an end to the steadying influence of the royal presence and royal patronage. Consequently, the earls met with no serious opposition. They were able to march through Kent with a growing force, and not even the Lancastrian garrison in London could prevent the city fathers – after some understandable hesitation – from opening their gates to the rebels on 2 July. The Lancastrian lords were forced to take refuge in the Tower of London, whence they bombarded the city, to the fury of its people.

Control of London, the administrative and financial centre of the realm, was clearly an invaluable asset to the invaders, but they could not hope to be secure or to command any general authority until the king's forces had been defeated in the field. Moreover, they were still proscribed rebels and traitors with no authority to rule. Still

Opposite: battle at sea; from *The Beauchamp Pageant,* c. 1485–90.

45

vehemently protesting that they had come only to gain a hearing from the king, and taking with them a whole covey of prelates (headed by the Archbishop of Canterbury) to mediate on their behalf, they set forth from London only two days later to seek out Henry VI in the Midlands.

The royalists had not been inactive. The king had with him a number of Lancastrian notables, including the Duke of Buckingham (whose influence was successfully thrown against any parley with the rebels), the Earl of Shrewsbury, Viscount Beaumont and Lord Egremont, a younger son of the Earl of Northumberland. Together they had assembled a sizeable army at Northampton. There the two forces clashed on 10 July: the battle was largely decided by the timely treachery of Lord Grey of Ruthyn, commander of the Lancastrian vanguard. The fighting was all over in half an hour; the Lancastrian leaders were dead on the field; the hapless king became a prisoner of the rebels.

The capture of Henry VI was the most important consequence of the battle. Escorted back to London with every possible mark of dignity and respect, he now became as pliable an instrument for the Yorkists who surrounded him as he had been in the hands of his own court party. We cannot know whether duress was applied to secure his compliance, but we can guess that he had now so far lost touch with the world of *realpolitik* that he was willing enough to sign or do anything that was asked of him. Control of the king gave the Yorkists a legal sanction for their rule, and for the next three months, while the Duke of York inexplicably dallied in Ireland, the Yorkist earls ruled in Henry's name. Their authority was still far from complete, for the queen and the Prince of Wales were still at large. So too were the Duke of Somerset, the Earls of Devon and Wiltshire, and other bitter enemies of the rebel leaders. Much of northern and south-western England, and most of Wales and the Marches, did not accept the new government's directives, and plans were already being concerted by the queen and her friends to assemble a new army at Hull in preparation for a march on London. Most of the lords, too, were animated by a stubborn sentiment of loyalty to the person of Henry VI. More important, however, the rebels now controlled the machinery of government. Southern and eastern England, as well as London itself, generally accepted their authority; and it was possible to summon a Parliament to meet at Westminster on 7 October. The prime purpose of the Parliament was to reverse the sentences of attainder passed at Coventry and reinstate the Yorkist leaders as loyal subjects of the crown.

This fairly favourable situation was to be dramatically changed by the sudden and unpredictable action of Duke Richard of York. From the moment of his landing near Chester on about 8 September 1460, it became clear that he had come to claim the throne of England for himself, a move which seems to have taken even his closest supporters by surprise and filled them with dismay. On reaching

Opposite: into battle; *The Beauchamp Pageant* indicates some of the main elements of late fifteenth-century fighting.

47

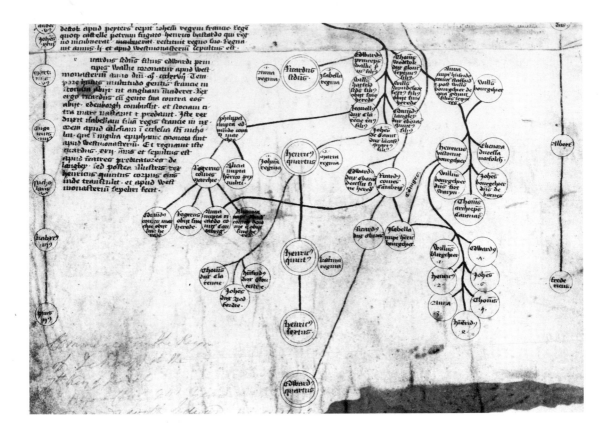

Legitimacy was an important part of the Yorkist claim to the throne. Here, the lower part of a genealogical roll, eighteen feet long, showing the descent of Edward IV from Jehosophat and the kings of Israel.

London, at the head of a pompous retinue, preceded by trumpeters bearing banners charged with the arms of England, and with his sword borne upright before him, in the manner of a king, he made his way to Westminster Hall where the Lords of Parliament were assembled. Then followed a startling and (for York) humiliating scene. Striding through the gathering in the hall, he made his way to the empty throne, laid his hand upon it (as though to claim it) for a few moments, and then turned to face the company, waiting for applause which never came. When the Archbishop of Canterbury suggested that he should go and see the king, he replied with the arrogant claim that 'I do not recall anyone I know within the kingdom whom it would not befit to come sooner to me and see me rather than I should go and visit him.' He then broke his way into the state apartments and 'lodged there for no little time more like a king than a duke'.

However high-handedly he might behave, York had once again sadly misjudged the political situation. Even Warwick and Salisbury were angry with him, and the Lords as a whole showed little sympathy with his demand that Henry VI should be deposed in his favour. He claimed to be the true king by right of descent from Lionel of Clarence – and he answered the Lords' objection, 'why then had he not borne the arms of Clarence but instead carried those of his paternal ancestor Edmund of Langley?', with the assertion that 'though right for a time rest and be put to silence, yet it rotteth not nor shall it perish'. But the Lords would have none of it, and placed themselves firmly upon the solemn oaths of loyalty which they had sworn to Henry as their rightful king. In the end a compromise was reached. On 10 October an Act of Accord recognized Henry as king for the rest of his natural life, but disinherited Edward, Prince of Wales, and vested the succession to the throne on the Duke of York and his sons after him. With this York had to pretend content.

There was, in any event, little scope for complacency in the Yorkist camp. Amid the prevailing political uncertainty law and order were gradually breaking down. In many regions, especially those remote from London, large bands of armed men roamed the countryside. In the hostile north the government had lost all semblance of authority, while on the border the King of Scots, always eager to exploit English weakness, had already captured the strongholds of Roxburgh and Wark and was threatening Berwick. More

The King of Scots: leader of a people whose views could never be completely discounted in English politics.

It was not only the common soldier who was at risk in fifteenth-century fighting.

serious still was the steady advance in the mobilization of the queen's forces. Early in December the Duke of Somerset and the Earl of Devon, at the head of their west-country retainers and tenantry, marched north to join Margaret at Hull, while from beyond the Trent the Duke of Exeter, the Earl of Northumberland and many tough and warlike northern barons came in to swell her forces.

The Yorkists responded promptly to the challenge. On 9 December Duke Richard, accompanied by the Earl of Salisbury and York's second son, Edmund, Earl of Rutland, left London for the north at the head of an army. His elder son, the Earl of March, was sent to Ludlow to crimp the activities of Jasper Tudor, Earl of Pembroke, and the Welsh Lancastrians, while Warwick and the Duke of Norfolk (one of the few non-Nevill magnates to support the Yorkists) remained behind in London. York reached his Yorkshire castle of Sandal, near Wakefield, in time for Christmas, and then on 30 December made his last and fatal miscalculation. With an army depleted by the absence of many men sent out on foraging patrols, he left the powerful protection of Sandal's mighty walls to challenge the queen's army, which was commanded by the sons of his former enemies and victims, Somerset, Northumberland and Clifford. The result was a rout. York was killed in the fighting. The young Earl of

The falcon and fetterlock, an emblem of Richard, Duke of York, father of Edward IV. His own bid for the throne ended in his defeat and death in December 1460.

Rutland (it was said) was stabbed to death by Lord Clifford on Wakefield Bridge. Salisbury was taken and soon after beheaded. The heads of York and Salisbury were impaled on the gates of the city of York, Duke Richard's adorned with the gruesome irony of a paper crown.

Margaret's triumph now opened the way for her troops to march south on London. The manner of her advance did her cause untold harm. Her troops were allowed to pillage and plunder at will, especially in places such as Grantham and Stamford, which formed part of the Duke of York's possessions. No doubt pro-Yorkist chroniclers and ballad-writers – with their tales of attacks on churches and the threat to southern womanhood from the licentious northerners – exaggerated. Nevertheless, the unbridled behaviour of the queen's troops sent a deep shiver of apprehension through the people of the southern counties, always fearful of northerners whom they regarded as wild and barbarous. Such apprehension later proved important, for fear of pillage was decisive in stiffening resistance in London after Margaret's second victory at St Albans on 17 February 1461. This bloody and bitterly fought encounter – one of the few battles for which we have a good eye-witness account – saw the total defeat of the Yorkist forces commanded by the Earl of

Warwick. Even more important, it changed the entire political situation, for that useful political vegetable, Henry VI, was now recaptured by his domineering queen. At once all legal sanction for the Yorkist regime was lost, and the wheel of dynastic revolution took a further and decisive turn, for now the Yorkists had no choice but to set up their own king in opposition to Henry.

Had Margaret of Anjou been able to re-establish herself in the capital in the days following her army's victory at St Albans, the course of the civil war might have been radically different. As it was, popular feeling in the city was running strongly against her. The authorities dithered between the awkward alternatives of refusing entry to a victorious army, which might wreak vengeance if defied,

The Sun in Splendour –
Edward IV's favourite badge
– seen on a frieze in St
George's Chapel, Windsor:
Edward was buried there in
the newly built choir.

and admitting troops who had already acquired an evil reputation
for licence. Their hesitation, stiffened by fear of popular reaction,
lasted long enough for Margaret to decide to withdraw northwards
and for the new white hope of York, Edward, Earl of March, to
enter the city at the head of a victorious force. The eighteen-year-old
Edward was fresh from his triumph over Jasper Tudor and the
Welsh Lancastrians at the Battle of Mortimer's Cross in the Welsh
Marches (2 or 3 February 1461) – a battle about which we know
little apart from its meteorological appendices, three suns 'in the
firmament shining full clear'. These were interpreted by Edward
as a portent of victory, and from them he seems to have derived his
favourite personal badge – the Sun in Splendour or the golden

sunburst, which still today rises triumphant in the roof-bosses of the sanctuary at Tewkesbury Abbey, in St George's Chapel at Windsor, and in the pages of many a Yorkist manuscript.

Unsullied by the taint of defeat which hung over Warwick, and confident in his own personal destiny, Edward of March now proceeded to have himself proclaimed and installed as king (4 March 1461). Here again possession of the capital was of vital importance, for any ceremony of king-making which did not make use of Westminster Abbey and of the traditional panoply of rightful rule would have totally lacked conviction. No shadow-ceremony conducted in Ludlow or anywhere else could have commanded the same authority. Edward was shrewd enough to emphasize the traditional forms and ceremonies – no jot or tittle of the making of a king was omitted, even though he still lacked support from a majority of the nobility.

Those modern historians who have represented Edward as merely a puppet in the hands of the great Earl of Warwick, and the whole affair as something stage-managed by the Kingmaker, have gravely misunderstood the political realities of March 1461. For better or for worse, Edward already knew his own mind; he would not accept dictation from his mighty cousin of Warwick. The army which provided the ultimate physical sanction for Edward's proclamation as king was a Yorkist force drawn from the Welsh and Marcher estates of his father, Duke Richard; the men who were to loom large in the politics of the 1460s – men like William Hastings and William Herbert, later Earl of Pembroke – already stood at Edward's side; and these were men who had served the House of York and owed no loyalty to a temporarily mute and inglorious Warwick. Edward's assumption of the crown in March 1461 was the first public assertion of his own forceful personality. If Warwick had possessed more political intuition he would have recognized the signs that the new king was to be his master not his disciple.

There was small time to linger over the crown-wearing ceremonies and the subsequent banquets. The formal coronation of the new king was postponed until it could be consecrated by the blessing of military victory over the Lancastrian forces – and God, said the Yorkist propaganda, was firmly on the side of England's new saviour, The Rose of Rouen. The speed and vigour with which Edward mounted his northern campaign of 1461 are symptomatic of the energy which the young king brought to all his affairs. Sending his lieutenants out of London to raise troops, collecting money by loans from reluctant Londoners, Edward had an army on the march from London by 13 March 1461. By the time he reached Pontefract in Yorkshire (27 or 28 March), moving by deliberate stages to allow recruits to flow in, he commanded an exceptionally large army by the standards of the time. Nor had his enemies been laggard in recruiting men, for Henry VI still attracted the loyalty of a majority among the English nobility. When the two armies

finally clashed at Towton, on Palm Sunday, 29 March 1461, in the bitter weather of a Yorkshire spring, their joint numbers may have exceeded 50,000 men – the largest set-piece battle of the entire civil war. Details of the battle are discussed below (Chapter 4), and for the moment it is enough to say that it resulted in an overwhelming Yorkist victory. At the end of the day the flower of the northern nobility and gentry lay dead on the field, or were taken prisoner and executed soon after. Prominent among the exceptionally large casualty list on the Lancastrian side were the young heads of strong Lancastrian families, like the Earls of Northumberland, Devon and Wiltshire. Although such stalwarts as Somerset and Exeter and Lord Roos made good their escape, the importance of the battle lay in the fact that it finally shattered the strength of the great northern families who had hitherto been loyal to Lancaster. Towton finally persuaded many nobles that it was no more than prudent and sensible to make peace with the new king. Not for a decade were the Lancastrian loyalists able to confront Edward IV again in an encounter of this scale.

Within a few months of Towton Edward IV effectively established himself as master of the realm. In Wales Lancastrian resistance soon crumbled against a vigorous campaign led by William, Lord Herbert. Only the great coastal fortress of Harlech held out – for no

The lustre of a Westminster Abbey coronation had long been a necessity in king-making: a manuscript of *c.* 1460–80 looks back to that of Henry IV.

Harlech Castle: a constant
(and virtually impregnable)
reminder to Edward IV of
his Lancastrian enemies. It
was finally reduced in 1468.

less than seven years – largely because the Yorkists did not want the
expense of a set siege of this virtually impregnable stronghold.
Isolated rebel intrigue in the west country and elsewhere quickly
came to an end as the leaders were rounded up, and were either
executed or submitted themselves to the king's grace. Only in the
far north-east of England did Lancastrian activity continue on any
significant scale.

The problem here was a complicated one. Henry VI and his supporters were sheltered and aided by the Scots, and to a lesser extent
by the French. The region itself was remote, difficult of access, and
dominated by great fortresses like Alnwick, Bamburgh and Dunstanburgh. Such strongholds could be reduced only by the lengthy
process of investment and starving the garrisons into surrender, or

by the even more expensive business of an artillery bombardment.
Above all, this was Percy country. Even in the sixteenth century, it
could be said that Northumberland knew no king but a Percy. For
the time being, the family's fortunes lay in ruins. The 2nd earl had
fallen at 1st St Albans in 1455; the 3rd earl died at Towton; the
young heir, later recognized as 4th earl, was prisoner in the Tower.
The family estates had been confiscated and were divided up among
Warwick, Warwick's brother John Nevill (Lord Montagu) and the
king's brother, George, Duke of Clarence. Even so it was hard to
break the region's traditional loyalty to the Percy cause. In the attempt
to win the support of Percy tenants and retainers, Edward was reduced
to the desperate expedient of seeking the goodwill of, for example,
Sir Ralph Percy, a younger son of the 2nd earl, even to the extent

The northern strongholds of
Bamburgh (*left*) and
Dunstanburgh (*below*): the
loyalties of those in
command of such fortresses
were often as important as
their military defences.

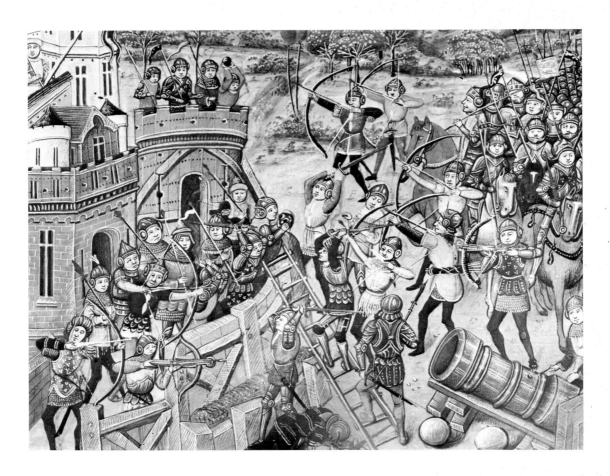

of entrusting him with the command of one or more of the key northern strongholds. Given the lethal harm done to the Percies by the House of York, the loyalty of a man like Sir Ralph had at best the brittle quality of thin ice, as Edward discovered to his cost. Appointed Captain of Dunstanburgh in autumn 1461, he speedily surrendered it to Queen Margaret when she landed in 1462; yet when it fell to the Yorkists at Christmas, he was nevertheless pardoned and reappointed Captain, and was given Bamburgh also, only to turn his coat again in March 1463. Probably because of the enormous expense involved, and his own acute financial problems, Edward seems never to have considered the alternative of stocking the castles with really strong garrisons under dependable captains.

These difficulties explain the bewildering shifts in military fortunes in the north-east and the long series of alarums and excursions which it caused the Yorkist government. No sooner, it seemed, was all well than all was ill again. In the autumn of 1461 the Yorkist captains, Warwick and Montagu – for Edward IV personally took no part in these northern campaigns – gradually obtained the submission of the far north. Alnwick surrendered in mid-September and Dunstanburgh soon after. Even so, a Lancastrian raid under Sir

Attack upon a castle. Frontal assaults like this were rare in the Wars of the Roses. In besieging the great Northumbrian strongholds (*opposite*) the tendency was to starve the garrisons into surrender.

Louis XI of France, the arch-enemy of Edward IV.

Opposite: contemporary English representation of a knight and archers, *c.* 1480. Both longbows and crossbows are shown.

William Tailboys recaptured Alnwick during the winter, and another rebel, Humphrey, Lord Dacre, slipped across the western border and retook his family stronghold of Naworth, near Carlisle. Not until the following summer, during a short truce with Scotland, did Naworth fall once again into Yorkist hands; it was only then, too, that Alnwick surrendered after a siege by Lord Hastings and Sir John Howard. As so many modern wars of independence have demonstrated, the support and sympathy of the local population worked against what was regarded as a hostile government, and enabled even small forces of active rebels to defy it for months on end.

Soon Queen Margaret descended on the scene, in her most determined effort to challenge the new dynasty in England. At the cost of promising him the English stronghold of Calais, she had persuaded the wily and ambitious Louis XI of France to grant her aid by the secret agreement of Chinon (24 June 1462). His enthusiasm soon cooled when he found he could not in practice retake Calais without taking on the Duke of Burgundy also. In the end Margaret was able to collect only a modest force of 800 men under her devoted friend, Pierre de Brézé. Yet even this tiny army exposed the brittle quality of Yorkist control in the north-east of England. When she landed near Bamburgh Castle on 25 October, dangerously late in the campaigning season, Bamburgh, Dunstanburgh and Alnwick soon opened their gates, and Northumberland was once more out of government control.

Edward's rapid response showed his deep alarm. Almost the entire nobility of England was summoned to his side, including 2 dukes, 7 earls, 31 barons and 59 knights. A contemporary writer, who was one of the host, claimed that the king commanded between thirty and forty thousand men. Alarmed by the advance of this army, and dismayed by the failure of her cause to attract much general support

Incipit secundus magne historie liber de conquesti.

Storm at sea: one of many
hazards to be faced when a
throne was at stake.

outside the north-east, Margaret decided to seek safety in Scotland.
Garrisons remained in the Northumbrian castles, but the queen and
her French followers took ship for Berwick on 13 November 1462.
Winter storms attacked her ships. Margaret and De Brézé managed
to reach Scotland safely, but the Frenchmen were driven ashore at
Lindisfarne and either slaughtered or taken captive by the king's
men. Soon afterwards the royal army reached the north and proceeded to invest the rebel strongholds. Edward himself got no
further than Durham, where he fell ill of measles. Overall command
fell to Warwick, who conducted the operations by means of a daily
round on horseback from a base at Warkworth. The king was reluctant to destroy the castles by gunfire, so the plan was to starve the
garrisons into surrender.

This was a remarkable operation for the place and the season of
the year. Tough, hardy and used to discomfort as they were,
medieval soldiers had a deep distaste for winter campaigning, and
naturally preferred the mulled wine (or mulled ale) and log fires of
their homes to the chilly miseries of tents and siege-works. That

A siege: from a manuscript of *c.* 1470.

harsh disciplinarian, Henry V, had forced his armies to maintain winter sieges in northern France, but no one had yet attempted them in the even bleaker conditions of Northumbria in December. Desertions from the Yorkist lines were frequent, in spite of the threat of the death penalty for absconders. Still the Yorkist armies held together, and the garrisons of Bamburgh and Dunstanburgh, who are said to have been reduced to eating their horses, offered to surrender on Christmas Eve. A Scots army was by now coming up to their relief, but this fact may not have been known to the defenders. Alnwick, however, held out. When the Scots appeared near by, Warwick agreed to allow the garrison under Lord Hungerford to march out and join them. Perhaps he feared to risk a fight, for his troops were suffering miseries from cold and rain and their morale was low, but some contemporaries implied a certain cowardice on his part. Certainly, as a commander, he lacked the aggression and boldness which distinguished his cousin Edward IV.

Yorkist occupation of the three Northumbrian strongholds proved short-lived. In April 1463 Sir Ralph Percy turned his coat

Henry VI, appropriately
removed from the scene of
battle, on a stained-glass
window at King's College
Chapel, Cambridge.

again, and let the Lancastrians into Bamburgh and Dunstanburgh. The former Lancastrian Captain of Alnwick, Sir Ralph Grey, had agreed to serve under a Yorkist superior, Sir John Astley, but he remained discontented. Soon Astley was seized, and the castle turned over to Henry VI's supporters. Northumberland passed out of government control, and for a time even Newcastle seemed in danger. Alarming news flocked back to London from Warwick and Thomas, Lord Stanley, who had been sent to investigate, for this time the rebels were to have the backing of a large invasion army of Scots, led by the young king, James III, the Dowager-Queen of Scots, Mary of Guelders, Henry VI and Margaret of Anjou. In July 1463 they laid siege to the great border fortress of Norham on the Tweed. In London King Edward obtained a grant of taxation from Parliament on the promise that he would raise an army and lead it in person against the Scots, an undertaking which he signally failed to keep. In fact, Warwick and Montagu, with aid from the Archbishop of York and a force of northern levies, confronted the Scots, who abandoned the siege of Norham and fled. The Nevills followed up with a punitive raid into Scotland, pillaging and burning for some sixty miles north of the border, but no further effort was made to reduce the Northumberland strongholds, even though the king spent much of the autumn of 1463 in Yorkshire.

In the closing months of that year the prospects of the rebels slowly deteriorated. Edward IV rightly divined that the best way to overcome their stubborn resistance was to deprive them of foreign support, and bent all his considerable diplomatic energy to that end. In October King Louis of France agreed to a truce and specifically renounced all future aid to Henry VI and his party. The Scottish government followed suit in December, and plans were made for a more permanent settlement, to be negotiated at Newcastle in March 1464. Henry VI had to leave Edinburgh and take up residence instead at Bamburgh. The Lancastrians now made a final effort. Led by the Duke of Somerset, who after a temporary honeymoon with Edward IV, had returned to his true allegiance, they did their best to stir up anti-government risings in Wales, Lancashire and Cheshire. Since they still faced no organized resistance in the north-east, they carried out a series of raids from Bamburgh and laid siege once more to Norham Castle. Finally, in an attempt to stop the Anglo-Scottish negotiations, they set out to ambush Lord Montagu, who had been sent north to the border to escort the Scots envoys to York. Montagu fought off the rebels under Somerset and Lords Roos and Hungerford in an engagement at Hedgeley Moor, near Alnwick, on or about 25 April 1464, and the tiresome Sir Ralph Percy was killed. While Edward, now again very short of money, made rather leisurely preparations to raise an army for the subjugation of the north, the invaluable Montagu cracked the kernel of the Lancastrian nut for him. The rebels' position was now increasingly desperate, and, if they were to retain credibility and support, they urgently needed at least some local success. Hearing that they were mustering their forces in Tynedale at the end of April, Montagu set out again, aided by Lords Greystroke and Willoughby, and, with a force of perhaps 4,000 men at most, fell upon them near Hexham (15 May 1464). The result was a rout. Most leading rebels were either taken on the field or soon afterwards, and were soon put to death in the round of executions which followed. Somerset, Roos and Hungerford died in this way. Another obdurate rebel, Sir William Tailboys, was captured in a coalpit near Newcastle, with considerable sums of Lancastrian war-funds in his pockets: he too shared the fate of the others. Only Henry VI, who had not been near the battlefield, made good his escape.

Montagu's conspicuous triumph spelt the end of Lancastrian resistance in the north. Deprived of their principal leaders, and faced by an advancing royal army with a great train of siege-cannon, the Lancastrian garrisons of the Northumberland castles had little incentive to go on fighting. Alnwick and Dunstanburgh surrendered on 23 May. Only Bamburgh, where the rebel commander, Sir Ralph Grey, could now hope for no mercy from the Yorkists, showed fight. Its refusal to surrender forced the Yorkists into the only set siege with artillery of the entire civil war. The great guns – valuable enough to have their own names, such as *Newcastle*, *London* and *Dijon* – soon broke breaches in the walls, and wounded Grey himself, his chamber being penetrated by a number of cannon-balls. Under this murderous fire the castle finally surrendered, and the wounded Grey was led off to execution.

The prolonged resistance of even small forces in Northumberland and at Harlech illustrates the difficulty which a government faced in suppressing rebellions in the more remote parts of the realm, particularly when they enjoyed the sympathies of the local population. But they never succeeded in attracting more general support. Most men had now accepted the reality of Yorkist control. Once the rebels were deprived of foreign backing, their cause was doomed.

YORK DIVIDED 1469–71

If Richard Nevill, Earl of Warwick, had been a man of different temperament, there need never have been any further extension of civil war in England. The Lancastrian cause was now so crushed and discredited that it had no hope of revival unless the victorious Yorkists quarrelled among themselves and one faction sought refuge under the banner of Lancaster. Warwick was himself primarily to blame for this development.

Warwick and his family had been most lavishly rewarded by Edward for the invaluable services they rendered to the Yorkist dynasty during the take-over of power in 1460–61 and the subsequent fighting in the north. The earl himself became Admiral of England, Great Chamberlain, Captain of Calais, Constable of Dover

Siege-cannon – a prominent feature in this scene from a manuscript made for Edward IV – were in practice much larger and more formidable than the artist represents them.

and Warden of the Cinque Ports, and received a host of other offices, wardships and grants of land. His uncle, William Nevill, Lord Fauconberg, was made Earl of Kent and given great estates in the west country; one of his younger brothers, George Nevill, became Chancellor of England and Archbishop of York; the other, John Nevill (Lord Montagu), was created Earl of Northumberland in 1464 and became heir to the great Percy power in north-eastern England. By permission of the young king, Earl Richard was allowed an influence so commanding and conspicuous that some foreign observers formed the misleading impression that he was the real ruler of England. If, however, the earl believed that his young cousin would always be willing to accept his direction and control, then he gravely misjudged his man; and it was, above all, the steady erosion of his early influence over Edward which Warwick proved unwilling to accept.

From the first there were small but clear signs that Edward had a mind of his own. Early in the reign, for example, while making Warwick all-powerful in the north, he refused to allow him to pursue his plans for family aggrandizement in South Wales, an area which he had marked out for his own man, William Herbert, created Earl of Pembroke in 1468, who was to become a virtual viceroy in that region. Warwick soon had more substantial reasons for discontent. As a king, Edward had much to commend him. Exceptionally tall and well made, he had an imposing royal presence. Contemporaries believed him to be remarkably handsome, although one cannot deduce this from the rather flat features, narrow eyes and small mouth of his earliest surviving portrait. He had intelligence, wit, charm and energy, and his notorious devotion to the pleasures of the flesh was not allowed to interfere with an able conduct of his royal business. But he was also impetuous, and prone to serious political misjudgments. The first of these was Edward's impulsive and secret marriage in May 1464 to an indigent Lancastrian widow, Elizabeth Woodville. By any standards it was a most unsuitable match for a king – the fact that it was made in secret showed Edward's awareness that it was a misalliance – and it surprised and dismayed even his closest supporters. But it had further and more serious consequences. Not only did it scupper Warwick's pet plan for a marriage between his king and a French princess; it also involved Edward in the need to provide suitably for Elizabeth's large and needy family. These included her two sons by her first marriage, her five brothers and her six sisters. Provision was made for them, without seriously impoverishing the crown, since they were not given extensive estates. But a remarkable and rapid series of marriages allied the new queen's family with most of the great families of England, particularly with some of the 'new men', like William Herbert, who were now emerging under Edward's patronage. Some of these marriages are said to have angered the Earl of Warwick, particularly that of his aunt, the wealthy dowager, Katherine Nevill, Duchess of Norfolk, who had already survived three husbands and was well into her sixties: she was now compelled to accept in matrimony one of the queen's brothers, John Woodville, who was still in his teens.

More serious for Warwick, however, was that this scooping of the baronial marriage market for the benefit of the queen's relatives deprived him of suitable husbands for his own daughters, Isabel and Anne, now both approaching marriageable age. These young ladies were the greatest heiresses in England, whose rank and wealth deserved only the highest blood of the realm. There now remained only two appropriate husbands, Edward's younger brothers, George, Duke of Clarence, and Richard, Duke of Gloucester. Edward stubbornly set his face against any such alliances, which could only increase still further the already overweening power of the Nevills. The Woodville marriage and its consequences might

O ure moost goode and gracious. Quene Elizabeth:
Soder vnto this oure fraternite: Of oure blessid
lady. And modr of mercy. Sanct Mary virgyn the
modr of God :·

not of themselves have caused a breach between the king and the earl, for Warwick grimly concealed his distaste, but he could scarcely have done other than resent the steady growth in influence of the queen and her relatives. For the Woodvilles were a greedy and grasping family, and deeply jealous of their influence with the king. They drew into their orbit 'new men' such as William Herbert, Earl of Pembroke in 1468, and Humphrey, Lord Stafford, later Earl of Devon; and the result was the emergence of a court party which was of Edward's own creation and which was exclusively dependent on him for promotion and patronage. This faction, later denounced by Warwick as traitors, was naturally hostile to the earl's party, and soon came to command an influence at court which rivalled and overshadowed that of the Nevills. King Edward's brusque dismissal of Archbishop George Nevill from the chancellorship of England in 1467 was a clear announcement on his part that he would no longer accept the blustering control of the Nevills.

Domestic differences were inflamed by deep divisions between the king and the earl over the direction of English foreign policy. Warwick was a staunch advocate of an alliance with England's ancient enemy, France. If his hopes of sealing it with a dynastic marriage had been dashed, he did not give up hope of persuading Edward that it was still necessary and desirable. To some degree

Edward IV dining in state. From the *Black Book* (*c.* 1472), which laid down new regulations for the royal household.

Socrates: Edere oportet vt vivas non vivere vt edas

Rex erit invictvs fverit cvi copia victvs

Fifteenth-century courtly ceremony. Here, Louis XI presiding over a chapter of the Order of St Michael.

Warwick's own pride and ambition were involved, for the Machiavellian Louis XI of France successfully flattered the earl with promises of reward and power if he could bring off a firm Anglo-French alliance and prevent England drifting into a closer friendship with France's enemy and England's old ally, the Duke of Burgundy. For Warwick the French alliance soon became a touchstone of his power with the king. If he could not convince Edward, then clearly his period of dominance was at an end, and he would have to accept a subordinate role. But Edward, hesitantly at first, and then with greater resolution, moved steadily towards a connection with Burgundy. Treaties of commercial intercourse and of political alliance in 1467 were sealed, in the custom of the time, with a dynastic marriage, when Edward's sister, Margaret of York, became the third wife of Duke Charles the Bold of Burgundy. The marriage ceremonies in 1468, conducted with the maximum publicity, were the most splendid seen in Europe in the entire fifteenth century. Nor was it any consolation to Warwick that the Woodvilles had a hand in all this, for the queen's mother, Jacquetta, Duchess of Bedford, had connections of birth with the high Burgundian aristocracy, and a family often accused of being parvenu was naturally anxious to emphasize its links with one which could claim descent from the Emperor Charlemagne. The Burgundian alliance was as much a triumph for Woodville self-esteem as it was a defeat for Warwick.

Edward IV's sister, Margaret of York, whose marriage to the Duke of Burgundy, Charles the Bold, in 1468 took place amid scenes of great grandeur. Their initials, 'C' and 'M', can be seen (*below centre*).

The fifteenth-century Burgundian court of Charles the
Bold (*right*) and the other dukes of that line was one of
the most remarkable in the entire history of Europe;
below we see a feast-scene in a manuscript produced
for Charles's father, Philip the Good.

ter.
est.
regni.
sit.
rex.
regat.

Ps
lanta
coram
dno Kege
apud Westm

Warwick's deep chagrin over the collapse of his influence is reflected in his behaviour – a sulky retreat to his estates, a prickly refusal to collaborate in the preparations for the marriage, a series of dire warnings over the evil consequences of the new Burgundian alliance. It is to Edward's credit that he did all he could to allow the earl to retain a suitable honour and dignity even if it was clear that he could no longer make the major decisions. Every attempt was made to humour him; there was no effort to humiliate or belittle him; and the flow of royal favours continued undiminished until the very eve of his rebellion. But Warwick was not to be pacified. The main reason for the renewal of civil war in 1469 was Warwick's arrogant refusal to accept a subordinate role. Dignity without power was not for him. From late in 1468, if not earlier, he was actively planning a *coup d'état*.

His first move was to suborn the elder of the king's brothers, George, Duke of Clarence. In the Middle Ages, and indeed much later, the younger brothers of kings were only too often a thorn in the flesh of ruling monarchs. Given titles and lands, they were rarely entrusted with real power, and, because of their dynastic position, they usually became a focus for dissidence. In the same period, Louis XI of France suffered from the ambitions of his younger brother, Charles, Duke of Guienne, and James III of Scotland from his brother, Alexander, Duke of Albany. Clarence was no exception. Young, volatile and restless, he soon fell under the influence of Warwick's very considerable charm and powers of persuasion, and became a party to Warwick's secret intrigues at Rome to obtain a dispensation from the Pope allowing Clarence to marry the earl's elder daughter, Isabel. Whether Warwick initially intended to replace Edward on the throne by a more pliable Clarence, who would then be his son-in-law, is far from clear. The most immediate precedent for political take-overs, of which Warwick had direct personal experience, was to seize the person of the king, and then, while holding him in constraint, to rule in his name, as York had done after 1st St Albans and Warwick himself after the Battle of Northampton in 1460. But there was no harm in having the presumptive heir-male to the throne – for Edward IV and Elizabeth had as yet produced no son – on his side.

In the summer of 1469 the full extent of Warwick's treason became clear. Warwick, with his brother-in-law, the Earl of Oxford, slipped across to Calais for the celebration of Clarence's marriage to Isabel Nevill on 11 July – the service being conducted by George Nevill, Archbishop of York. At the same time, a series of risings developed in the north of England. Their chronology is confused and uncertain, and at least one of them seems to have been quite independent of the Nevill-inspired rebellions: this was a movement in the East Riding of Yorkshire, under a leader called Robin of Holderness, intended to restore the Percy family to its rightful place, but promptly suppressed by the Earl of Northumberland, Warwick's

Opposite:
Edward IV; a drawing – unique in showing him with a beard – on the King's Bench Plea Roll, Hilary Term, 1466.

77

Anthony Woodville, Lord Scales and 2nd Earl Rivers, a victim of Richard III, kneels to present a book to Edward IV and Queen Elizabeth Woodville. The future Edward V stands beside them.

brother, John Nevill. However, the major rebellion under a leader known as Robin of Redesdale was clearly the work of Warwick's agents, and had strong Nevill connections. Robin himself was probably Sir John Conyers, of Hornby in Yorkshire, who was Warwick's cousin by marriage, and among those later killed at the Battle of Edgecote (26 July 1469) were the earl's nephew, Sir Henry FitzHugh, and his cousin, Sir Henry Nevill, son of Lord Latimer. Yet if the hard core of the rebellion consisted of the many thousands of Nevill tenants and dependents, it also attracted much popular support elsewhere. Nevill propaganda plausibly and cleverly played on prevailing popular discontent: so far the Yorkist regime had done little to remedy the grievances which had made Henry VI's government so unpopular a decade before. It also appealed to popular vanity by making ominous comparisons with Edward II, Richard II and Henry VI, whose misdeeds had cost these kings their thrones, and by inviting the common people to make a 'remedy and reformation' of Edward IV's misguided government. This propaganda seems to have been successful in drawing many recruits to the rebel cause, and it was what southern chroniclers called 'a whirlwind from the north, a mighty insurrection of the commons' which began to march south from Yorkshire early in July.

Edward IV was very slow to react to these growing dangers. This was not the last occasion when he seemed reluctant to accept the fact of treason, and particularly the people's rejection of him. His disillusionment later led him, according to one foreign commentator, to give the order not to spare the commons in battle, for 'they loved him not'. From East Anglia, where he was on pilgrimage at the shrine of Walsingham, Edward made a somewhat leisurely journey north, via the York family house at Fotheringhay, where he rested for a few days or so, and eventually north through Grantham and Nottingham to Newark. There the news of the rebellion became unexpectedly ominous. He had not sufficient troops with him to challenge the rebels in arms, and desperate appeals to the city of Coventry and other towns to send him men as urgently as possible reflect his disarray. For the sake of their own safety, the unpopular Woodvilles, now more of a liability than an asset, were sent away – the queen's father, Richard Woodville, Earl Rivers, and one of her brothers, John Woodville, to Wales, and another brother, Anthony, Lord Scales, to Norfolk. By now Edward was beginning to admit to himself the treasonable behaviour of Warwick and Clarence, and on 9 July sent off to them rather wistful letters, asking them to come

William Herbert, 1st Earl of Pembroke, and his wife kneel before the enthroned Edward IV.

and show to him that they were not 'of any such disposition towards us, as the rumour here runneth'.

Events now moved swiftly to a climax. Warwick and Clarence had crossed to England after the wedding, were admitted to London by an anxious city government, and soon were marching north with a growing force to make junction with Redesdale's army advancing south, which had now by-passed the king at Nottingham. Edward's principal lieutenants, William Herbert, Earl of Pembroke, with a powerful force of Welshmen, and Humphrey Stafford, newly created Earl of Devon, with his west-country troops, were themselves moving rapidly north to the king's aid. The two armies, royalist and rebel, converged near Banbury. The resulting clash, known as the Battle of Edgecote, seems to have been decided largely by an extraordinary quarrel between Pembroke and Devon on the previous evening about billeting arrangements in Banbury town. As a result, Devon, who had most of the archers with him, made camp some miles away from the Welshmen, who bore the brunt of the rebel attack the next morning. Nevertheless, it was a very hard-fought battle, as the heavy casualties among men of rank on both sides testify. Only when a small detachment of Warwick's men, under Sir John Clapham, appeared on the field, did the Welshmen (mistaking it for the advance guard of another army) finally break and were overwhelmed. Devon's troops seem never to have been effectively engaged. Warwick lost no time in taking his revenge on his enemies. Pembroke and Sir Richard Herbert, his brother, the Earls of Devon and Rivers, and John Woodville were all executed as soon as the earl could lay hands on them. Three days later, Edward IV himself, who had been deserted by almost all his men as soon as the news of Edgecote reached them, fell into Warwick's hands, and the earl's triumph was complete.

There now followed a brief period during which Warwick attempted, unsuccessfully, to re-create the pattern of government – through a captive king – which had served him so well in 1460. Edward was sent off under custody first to Warwick Castle, and then to Middleham; Warwick issued writs and mandates in his name. But the earl soon discovered that the circumstances were now very different. To the lords his cause was clearly one of naked self-interest and personal aggrandizement, and he could not command their effective loyalty. Moreover, many were Edward's men, who owed new titles, offices and forfeited lands to his favour, and had no particular love for Warwick. Even the earl's supporters among the common people were probably bewildered and dismayed. They had supported him to see the king's unpopular favourites removed from power, and in the hope of some 'reformation of the realm' (which was not forthcoming), but they had probably not expected to see the king placed under physical duress and his power abrogated for the earl's benefit. Warwick's rule, therefore, lacked conviction and did not command general acceptance. As soon as a crisis blew

The sternly regular troop-lines on the manuscript battle-scene were often far removed from the actuality of disorder and confusion.

up – in the form of a Lancastrian rising on the northern border – it became clear that only the authority of the king in person could secure obedience. Warwick had no choice but to release Edward, and from about mid-September the king was back in control.

The position was now one of deep political unease. Edward could not be expected to forgive or forget the earl's rebellion, Clarence's treason or Warwick's wanton execution of Edward's father-in-law and brother-in-law and of valued and trusted supporters like Pembroke and Devon. He was scarcely likely ever again to place any trust in Warwick, and even to accept Clarence to his bosom meant a considerable act of faith. But Edward also needed time to re-create his own power-base. The court party on which he had relied now lay in ruins, with many of its members dead, and Warwick and Clarence still commanded a sufficient following to make it dangerous to challenge them openly. For this reason there was a superficial amity. Sir John Paston reported that 'the king himself hath good language of the Lords of Clarence, of Warwick, and of my Lords of York [Archbishop Nevill] and Oxford, saying they be his best friends', but, he added, 'his household men have other languages.'

Behind the scenes Edward worked steadily towards strengthening his own support and weakening and isolating Warwick and Clarence. In Wales he now placed much of the power and responsibility enjoyed by the late Earl of Pembroke on the shoulders of his younger brother, Duke Richard of Gloucester, who for the first time began to emerge as a political figure and, unlike Clarence, was noticeably loyal to Edward. In the north he planned to offset Nevill power by restoring the Percy heir, Henry Percy, to the earldom of Northumberland, but at the same time he sought to keep the loyalty of Warwick's brother, John Nevill (who lost his earldom of Northumberland), by promoting him (in March 1470) to the marquisate of Montagu, giving him extensive estates in the west country, and by marrying his eldest daughter, Elizabeth, to John's son, George Nevill, whom he created Duke of Bedford. He also sought to build up his support among the powerful families of Bourchier and Stafford. When trouble developed again early in 1470, Edward was ready for it, and was not caught unprepared a second time.

The origins of the rebellion which broke out in Lincolnshire in the early months of 1470 are obscure, but it seems to have sprung from a local feud between Sir Thomas Burgh, a prominent member of Edward IV's household, and a neighbouring nobleman, Richard, Lord Welles and Willoughby, and his son, Sir Robert Welles. It soon spread to present an open challenge to the king's authority. Clarence and Warwick seem to have been deeply implicated from the beginning, but on this occasion they achieved no element of surprise. Edward soon had the Lincolnshire leaders under lock and key; the rebel host, attempting to join Warwick near Leicester, was cut off and dispersed on 12 March at Lose-Cote Field near Stamford (so called because the rebels cast away their jackets in their haste to escape the field). Simultaneous risings planned for Yorkshire and the west country never got off the ground, and melted away as soon as the news of the king's victory reached them. At Lose-Cote Field the complicity of the duke and the earl had become apparent, for the rebels had used as their battle-cry 'A Clarence! A Clarence! A Warwick!' Later on, Edward was able to extract from Sir Robert Welles, shortly before his execution, a confession that Warwick and Clarence were 'partners and chief provokers of all their treasons', and that the rising had been planned to put Clarence on the throne. Finally, the refusal of the duke and the earl to answer repeated summons from the king to come before him and explain themselves made their guilt painfully apparent. On 24 March, the king, now at York, was able to denounce them publicly as traitors, and a price was put on their heads.

Clarence and Warwick, now thoroughly isolated, fled first to Lancashire, where they hoped in vain for the support of the shifty Stanley. They then made off in haste towards the south-west, pursued by the king, whose forces rode the 290 miles from York to Exeter in eighteen days. But he was too late. Taking with them the

This illumination, from a Flemish manuscript specially commissioned by him, probably shows Edward IV in exile in Holland (1470–71). The figure, second from left, with the Garter below his knee, may be the future Richard III.

Countess of Warwick and her daughters, they took ship from Devon for Calais, hoping to be admitted into the fortress (as in 1459). The commander at Calais, Warwick's deputy, John, Lord Wenlock, was an ally of theirs. Wenlock, however, felt it unsafe for them to enter, for Calais (he said) was a mousetrap; the Duchess of Clarence gave birth to a still-born child as the ships lay in the bay; and after a successful piratical attack on a Burgundian fleet in the Calais Roads, the rebel fleet withdrew south to seek refuge with King Louis XI in France.

Edward IV owed his victory in 1470 partly to his own vigilance and speed of action, so much in contrast to his dilatory complacency in 1469. The rebel scheme to distract him by simultaneous risings in different parts of the country, so that he would not know where to strike first, misfired through the rapidity with which he dispersed the Lincolnshire rebellion. Moreover, Warwick and Clarence had become by now politically isolated among the nobility, who stood solid for Edward. The duke and the earl did attract support from a number of substantial gentry, some of them with strong former

Lancastrian associations: after the leaders' flight to France Edward ordered the lands and property of no less than fifty-three of their supporters to be seized. But the nobility had remained unmoved by the manifest self-interest and ambition of the rebel cause. Even Warwick's own brother, John Nevill, Earl of Northumberland, had not supported them, although his loyalty was soon to be shaken by Henry Percy's restoration to his ancestral earldom of Northumberland on 12 March. Despite his marquisate, John evidently felt himself ill-used, and later in the year proved that he was no longer Edward's loyal servant.

The landing of Warwick and Clarence in France gave Louis XI the opportunity for what he obviously felt was his diplomatic masterstroke. Summoning up the ex-queen, Margaret of Anjou, from her refuge in eastern France, he persuaded her to agree to accept her former and bitter enemies as new allies. With French aid, the duke and the earl were to cross to England, drive out Edward IV, and restore Henry VI to the throne. When all was secure, Queen Margaret (who was not prepared to risk the safety of her precious son on any precarious adventure) would follow with Edward, Prince of Wales. This unholy alliance was sealed by a marriage – between Prince Edward and Warwick's younger daughter, Anne Nevill. As father-in-law of the heir to the throne, and father of the next queen, his future political security would be assured.

No such prospect existed for the Duke of Clarence. Brother, and still heir-male presumptive, of the king it was planned to depose, and now no longer himself an alternative candidate for the throne, he was in an ambivalent position to say the least. He was also compelled to promise to surrender to the queen many Duchy of Lancaster estates which had been settled on him by King Edward. Many other parts of his landed possessions belonged to former Lancastrian supporters, which they would expect to recover against him in due course. A Lancastrian restoration offered Clarence nothing but loss of power and wealth and an acutely uncomfortable political future. Not surprisingly he was later to become a focus for a series of approaches from Edward IV (then in exile) to abandon his course of treachery and return to the true allegiance of York. With Clarence a somewhat reluctant partner, therefore, the way was set for yet another sudden and dramatic reversal of political fortune.

The rebel invasion succeeded with surprising ease. Edward IV had allowed himself to be drawn away to the north to suppress a pro-Nevill rising in Yorkshire. Perhaps this was a strategic mistake, but the experience of 1469 had proved that these northern risings, if not swiftly nipped in the bud, could get altogether out of hand. He had also taken precautions to keep naval forces at sea to patrol the Channel and intercept any projected invasion from France. It was his misfortune that severe autumn gales scattered the royal ships

Opposite: Richard III's prayer book. We can judge from the date (*c.* 1440) that it was not commissioned for him; indeed, he was (unlike Edward IV) no great patron of the arts.

and gave Warwick's fleet the opportunity for an unimpeded crossing. In any event, Edward was still lingering in the north (weeks after FitzHugh's rebellion had collapsed) when Warwick and Clarence landed in Devonshire in mid-September. They were warmly received, for this was a part of the country which had strong Lancastrian loyalties, and where Clarence had extensive estates. Joined by the Earl of Shrewsbury and Lord Stanley with substantial retinues, they marched towards Coventry with a growing force.

In the north Edward suddenly found himself menaced by Montagu, and was deserted by most of his troops. Though he had still in his company a number of loyal noblemen, including his younger brother (Gloucester), Lord Hastings and Anthony Woodville, Earl Rivers, they had no opportunity to raise men, and decided that safety lay in immediate flight. A dash across Lincolnshire and over the Wash brought Edward to King's Lynn, where Rivers' influence enabled them to find shipping. On 2 October they set sail for the Low Countries and, after a perilous voyage, landed on the Dutch coast near Alkmaar. So hasty had been their flight, and so short of funds were they, that their shipmen had to be rewarded with gifts of clothing and personal jewellery. Fortunately for them, they were hospitably and graciously received by the Duke of Burgundy's Governor of Holland, Louis of Bruges, Lord Gruthuyse, who had several times been an ambassador to England and knew the king personally. Edward was later to reward Louis of Bruges's friendly concern by creating him Earl of Winchester in 1472: he was one of only three foreigners to receive an English peerage in the entire fifteenth century.

The restored government of Henry VI, which dated its acts from the beginning of October 1470, obviously rested upon uneasy political foundations. Some Yorkist peers could not be trusted and were placed in custody for a while. More serious were the potential tensions between the majority of moderate Yorkist lords and the returning or re-emerging Lancastrian nobility. The forfeited lands of the latter were now occupied by the former, and it was difficult to satisfy the one without antagonizing the other. There was not much available in the way of office or land with which to buy loyalty, and Warwick himself took some of the plums. Some of the old-guard Lancastrians, like the Duke of Somerset, had little love for Warwick and Clarence, and were merely awaiting the return of their true leaders, Queen Margaret and Edward, Prince of Wales, which was persistently delayed by adverse winds in the Channel.

Even so the new regime might have lasted much longer than it did had not Louis XI, unwisely and impatiently, begun to demand the price of his support for the Lancastrian restoration. Louis' most cherished political objective was the destruction of the independent state of Burgundy, and it had been a condition of his backing for Warwick that England should declare war upon Burgundy as soon as possible, and join him in a joint offensive against Duke Charles.

Louis of Bruges, Lord Gruthuyse, Governor of Holland for the Duke of Burgundy, who sheltered Edward IV and his friends during their enforced exile (1470–71).

In December 1470 he had declared war on Burgundy. On 12 February 1471 England followed suit, and orders were given to the garrison in Calais to start hostilities against the duke's territories near by.

England's new hostile posture had an immediate and dramatic effect on the attitude of Duke Charles of Burgundy. Not wishing to be embroiled in war at this stage, he had thus far preserved a most careful and punctilious neutrality towards the new government in England, and had pointedly ignored the presence in his dominions of his refugee brother-in-law. Edward now at once became an asset, for his successful restoration would knock out England as an ally of a permanently hostile France. Just as French backing had made possible the restoration of Henry VI, so Burgundian aid was a vital initial support for Edward's recovery of the throne in 1471. This was the second occasion during the Wars of the Roses when the great continental conflict between France and Burgundy decisively influenced the civil conflict in England. It was not to be the last, for again in 1485 and 1487 the attitudes of foreign powers made feasible attempts on the English throne.

Duke Charles now began to supply Edward with money, ships and a few hundred men. At the same time Edward made peace with the great German-Baltic trading confederation known as the Hanseatic League, with which his government had been on hostile terms since 1468, by promising to restore their privileges on his return, and the Hansards also supplied him with fourteen ships. Edward's agents were also making approaches to potential supporters in England, particularly Clarence, and the new Percy Earl of Northumberland, who, after all, owed his restoration to Edward, and had some reason to fear that under the new regime he might lose his earldom again to Warwick's brother, Montagu. Thus prepared, Edward organized his invasion fleet and set sail from Flushing on 11 March 1471.

With some 36 ships and about 1,200 men, part English, part Flemish, it was a tiny force by modern standards, but so, too, were all these seaborne invasions of the civil war, with the exception of Henry Tudor's expedition in 1485. Success depended essentially on raising support once a landing had been achieved. For Edward this was no easy matter. He would have preferred to descend on East Anglia, where he might hope for help from the Dukes of Norfolk and Suffolk, and where Earl Rivers had estates. But when the little fleet put in at Cromer on 12 March, and local men were put ashore to make inquiries, they reported that it would be quite unsafe to land. Edward's friends were in custody, and the Earl of Oxford had the region sewn up tight against him. He now had no choice but to retrace the steps of another successful pretender, Henry Bolingbroke in 1399, and make north to achieve a landing at Ravenspur inside the mouth of the Humber estuary.

Bolingbroke, however, had landed in a Yorkshire dominated by his own great estates, and where he could expect active support from the other great lords of the region, the Earls of Northumberland and Westmorland. In contrast, Edward encountered a largely hostile countryside. He had no support from the once-great Lancastrian connection. Montagu, no longer a friend, was at large, with his base at Pontefract Castle. Even when Edward reached his own family estates near Wakefield recruits were still far fewer than he had hoped for. Not even the sympathetic Earl of Northumberland could persuade his followers to take up arms on Edward's behalf. He did, however, perform an invaluable service to Edward in keeping them at home while the king was still highly vulnerable, and probably his undeclared support for York exercised a severe restraint on Montagu's freedom of action, for the latter failed to attack Edward's feeble forces as they marched just south of Pontefract towards Wakefield.

Precariously, Edward survived. The mere fact of his survival encouraged his supporters, and recruits began to flow in as he moved south, his most important reinforcement coming from several thousands of Midlands men who responded to the call of Lord Hastings. If there was one clear political lesson to be learned from the repeated rebellions and invasions which punctuated the Wars of the Roses, it was the decisive importance of confronting risings at once and before they had time to gather strength. The longer they could remain in being, the stronger they became, drawing on the volatile loyalties of the common people. Often the mere presence of a hostile force in a particular region compelled the local gentry to join it from sheer self-preservation.

Never was this lesson more clearly taught than in 1471. Warwick perhaps relied too much on the ability of Montagu to deal with Edward in Yorkshire, but by not advancing north at once and confronting Edward while he was still weak, he threw away an important advantage. When eventually Edward reached Coventry,

Opposite: the landing of English ships, packed with soldiers; from the *Chronique d'Angleterre*, late fifteenth century.

where Warwick lay within the protection of the town walls, he had a force to be reckoned with, and Warwick's failure to give fight even then did his cause no good. Edward's continued success was now turning the screws upon the dubious loyalties of Clarence. Eventually the duke decided to throw in his lot with his brother, and Warwick lost his most important ally. Other lords, like Shrewsbury and Stanley, cautiously waited to see which way the wind might blow. Important Lancastrians, like Somerset and Devon, took off for the south coast to await the imminent arrival of Queen Margaret, and offered Warwick no active support.

Thus encouraged, Edward made the bold decision to leave Warwick and his forces in the rear, and march straight on London. Possession of the capital, he rightly calculated, would bring important advantages and attract more recruits, for there were in those parts, as the official chronicle says, 'his true lords, lovers, and servants . . . in great number'. In fact, soon after his entry into the city men like Sir John (now Lord) Howard and Humphrey Bourchier, Lord Cromwell, flocked to join his standard. Attempts by the Lancastrian leaders within the capital to rally support by parading the ageing Henry VI through the streets, clad in a dingy gown of blue velvet, and accompanied only by a meagre retinue, did his cause more harm than good. As one London observer acidly commented, it was 'more like a play than the showing of a prince to win men's hearts'. Many of the leading London citizens had a strong financial stake in Edward's recovery of the throne, and some, according to the French historian, Philippe de Commines, were influenced by their wives, who had their own private and personal reasons to welcome back the debonair and promiscuous young king. On 11 April, therefore, London opened its gates to the Yorkists, and Edward was reunited with his wife and shown the son she had borne him in her sanctuary at Westminster Abbey during his exile.

There then followed the whirlwind campaign (described in more detail in the next chapter) which, within the space of a month, brought him decisive victories over Warwick, Montagu and Oxford at Barnet (14 April), and over Queen Margaret's Lancastrian army, commanded by Edward, Prince of Wales, Somerset and Devon, at Tewkesbury (10 May). In the week following the battle, the Londoners, stiffened by the presence of Rivers, Essex, Arundel and other Yorkist lords within the city, for once closed their gates against a hostile army; they beat off the pro-Nevill rebellion stirred up in Kent and the south-east by Warwick's kinsman, the Bastard of Fauconberg (an illegitimate son of William Nevill, Earl of Kent), at the head of a force of soldiers from the Calais garrison and sailors from his own fleet. When the news of Tewkesbury reached the north, further pro-Nevill risings folded up, and on 14 April, at Coventry, the Earl of Northumberland came to inform Edward that the north was now quiet and anxious for the king's grace. When, therefore, Edward re-entered London in triumph on 21 May,

entre les autres maulx il
leur fist presque perdre la
saison. Et au regard de luy il
auoit son armee si rompue
si mal en point et si poure qil
ne losoit mõstrer deuãt eulx
car il auoit perdu deuant
mez quatre mil hõmes pre
nans soulde / entre lesquelz
y mourut des meilleures gẽs
quil eust. Et ainsi verrez

que dieu le disposa de tous
poïntz a faire contre la raiso
de ce que son affaire reque
roit / et contre ce quil sca
noit et entendoit mieulx q̃
mil autre dix ans auoit.

Cõment le roy Edouard
dangleterre passa en france
et descendit a Calaix pour
faire la guerre au roy / et
de ce qui en aduint.

attended by almost the entire surviving peerage of England, all effective resistance to his authority was at an end.

YORK AND TUDOR 1483–87

In the sense that they were a dynastic struggle between the Houses of York and Lancaster, the Wars of the Roses ended in 1471. The Lancastrian Prince of Wales had died in the fighting at Tewkesbury. His father, Henry VI, finally ended his unhappy life on the very night of Edward IV's return to London, and there is little doubt that he was murdered on Edward's orders. The troublesome ex-Queen Margaret, taken captive after Tewkesbury, was soon ransomed by Louis XI and was shuffled off to eastern France, where she died in poverty in 1482. There was now no respectable Lancastrian claimant to the English throne left alive if we exclude King John II of Portugal, who was descended from John of Gaunt, Duke of Lancaster, by his first wife Blanche. But, aside from the important fact that he was an alien, his claim came only through the female line, from his ancestress, Philippa, daughter of John and Blanche.

One remotely potential claimant survived in the person of Henry Tudor, the future Henry VII, an obscure and penniless refugee living in Brittany in the care of his faithful uncle, Jasper Tudor, the Lancastrian Earl of Pembroke. His claim was, in any case, extremely weak, since it came through his mother, Margaret Beaufort. The Beauforts were originally the bastard children of John of Gaunt by his mistress, later his third wife, Catherine Swynford. They had been legitimated by Act of Parliament in Richard II's reign, but the first Lancastrian king, Henry IV, had added a rider to a repeat of this legitimization, excluding them from succession to the throne. Whether Henry's declaration, for which he had no parliamentary sanction, was valid as against the earlier Act is doubtful, but the lack of full authority for Henry's exclusion clause may not have been generally known; and a large question-mark of dubiety hung over any claim based upon a Beaufort descent.

After Henry VII's marriage to Edward's eldest daughter, Elizabeth of York, Tudor propaganda made great play with the notion that they had thereby united the rival claims of Lancaster and York. Later it was said of Henry VIII that he was 'the indubitate flower and very heir' of Lancaster and York. Yet Henry VII himself was conspicuously careful in 1485 not to make any claim to the throne based upon a Lancastrian descent. He claimed, in effect, by right of conquest. His victory at Bosworth, he was to say, expressed the 'true judgment of God' and so gave him a kind of divine right. His first Parliament of 1485 avoided the question of title altogether and merely stated that, by authority of Parliament, it was ordained that the inheritance of the crowns of the realms of England and France rested in 'the most royal person of our now sovereign lord King Harry VII'. Henry Tudor was wise to make no specific claim by

Opposite: Margaret Beaufort, mother of Henry VII, who helped to promote the rebellion of 1483 against Richard III: a great patroness of education, especially at Cambridge.

93

descent, for there were many people alive in England in 1485 who had a far better claim to the throne by descent from Edward III (not necessarily through the Lancastrian line) than his own. For a long time to come, the public executioners of the first two Tudor kings were kept busy thinning the ranks of this 'royal race', usually, it should be said, because of the treachery and foolishness of their victims rather than as a result of any calculated royal policy of extinction.

In 1471, however, all this was far in the future and could not possibly have been foreseen. Henry Tudor was so totally unimportant politically that Edward IV made only the most half-hearted and sporadic attempts to obtain control of his person from the Duke of Brittany. Edward himself was to rule England for twelve more years in absolute dynastic security, until he died, powerful, wealthy and respected, at the early age of forty.

Once again only divisions within the ruling Yorkist party could have produced the renewal of civil war, since there was no threat from outside. Edward IV himself had contributed in no small measure to dissensions among his nobility. In particular, he showed excessive favour to the queen and her highly unpopular Woodville relatives. In 1478, they largely engineered the overthrow of the elder of Edward's brothers, George, Duke of Clarence, who was judicially murdered in the Tower of London – traditionally by drowning in a butt of malmsey wine. The Woodvilles also acquired more or less exclusive control of the heir to the throne, Edward, Prince of Wales, and his younger brother, Richard, Duke of York, over whom they exercised a commanding influence. This policy sat awry with Edward's other policy of steadily building up the power of his other brother, Richard, Duke of Gloucester, in the north of England. Married to the younger daughter of Warwick the Kingmaker, Anne Nevill, he soon became heir not only to Warwick's great north-country estates, but also to the loyalty and service of former Nevill servants and retainers in the regions beyond the Trent. Strengthened still further by lavish grants of estates and offices, he came to enjoy a power and a following in the north of an unprecedented kind. But, like many of the nobility, Richard hated, and was jealous of, the grasping Woodvilles, and feared a royal minority (Edward V was twelve when his father died in 1483) dominated by them. Moreover, as the king's nearest male relative, he was the natural choice to act as regent or protector of the realm in the event of a minority, something which the Woodvilles in their turn would do all in their power to oppose. The existence of these rivalries was what made possible Duke Richard's seizure of the throne in June 1483. Probably it was fear for his own safety and future which inspired his action, rather than any deep-laid plan or the determination 'to prove a villain' which Shakespeare and the Tudor tradition attributed to him. But in the circumstances his seizure of power could only be achieved by extremely violent

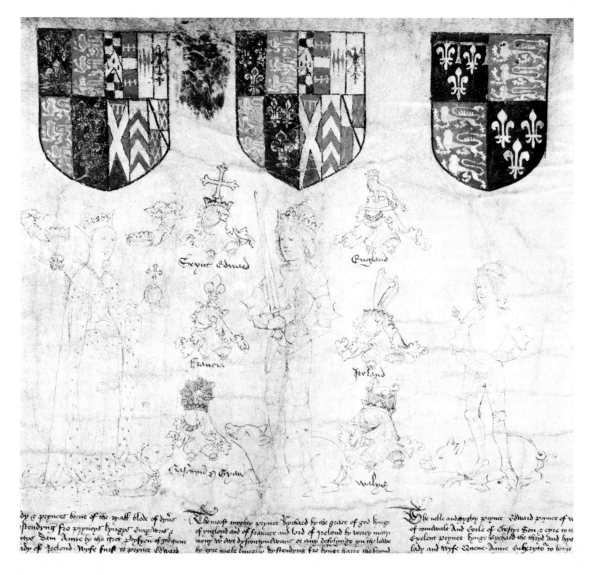

Richard III and his queen, Anne Nevill, with their son, Edward, who died in childhood.

means, and these seriously weakened the ruling Yorkist party and heightened the divisions within it.

Apart from justifying his claim to the throne by circulating a highly specious story (which no one believed) that the sons of Edward IV were bastards, Richard's seizure of power involved the judicial murders of the young king's uncle, Anthony Woodville, Earl Rivers, and of the queen's younger son by her first husband, Richard Grey; the execution without trial of Edward IV's most loyal supporter, the much-respected William, Lord Hastings, who could not be expected to tolerate Richard's plans to depose Edward's sons; and the imprisonment in the Tower of Edward V and his brother, where they soon – and ominously – disappeared altogether from public view.

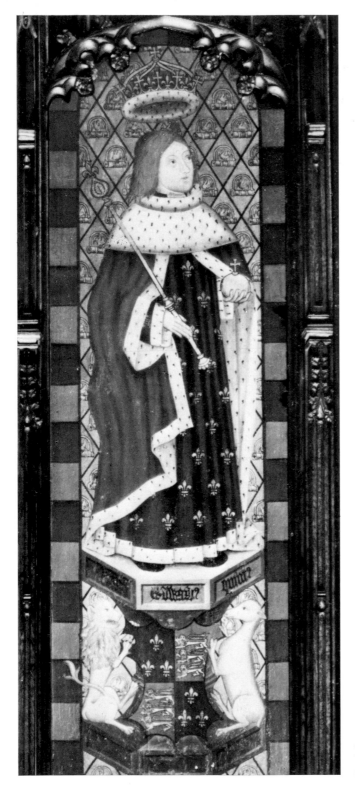

Edward V, whose mysterious disappearance as one of 'the Princes in the Tower' followed his uncle Richard III's seizure of power.

Such methods inevitably produced a reaction. Not only were the surviving Woodvilles necessarily driven into active conspiracy, but, more serious, Richard's cynicism and ruthlessness cost him the support of many of the leading gentry of southern and western England. Many of these were former servants of King Edward IV; they had close personal associations with his court and were loyal to the true Yorkist line. Within three months of Richard's accession, there were dangerous movements afoot in the southern counties to release the princes from their custody in the Tower. Soon rumours were spreading that the sons of Edward IV were already dead at their uncle's hand, and – whether rightly or wrongly – they were widely believed. The resentment and suspicion felt for Richard led the southern gentry into supporting a scheme to depose him in favour of the still unknown Henry Tudor, who was to marry Edward's eldest daughter, Elizabeth of York. This plot was probably hatched between Henry's mother, Margaret Beaufort, and the queen-dowager, Elizabeth Woodville – and the fact that the latter supported a scheme to put Henry Tudor on the throne is a telling indication that she believed her sons by Edward IV to be already dead. At some stage – perhaps from the very beginning – the plot was backed by Richard's principal supporter, Henry Stafford, Duke of Buckingham. His motives for rebellion were highly obscure even to his contemporaries, and are no more clear today; but his adherence converted the dissidence in the southern counties into a potentially most dangerous rising.

Richard III was now in something of a dilemma. If the princes were still alive and well, he might have produced them and thereby chopped the supports from the plan to make Henry Tudor king; but his doing so would not have contented the Yorkist loyalists who wished to see Edward V in his rightful place on the English throne. In the event, Richard did and said nothing about the princes, and thereby confirmed the general belief that he had had them put to death (a belief since accepted by the great majority of historians). Fortunately for Richard, the rebellion in practice did not match its potential. In Kent the risings went off at half-cock and prematurely, and John, Lord Howard (now Duke of Norfolk), was able to secure London and alert his master. In Wales Buckingham himself was hampered by his own unpopularity with his Welsh tenantry, which made it difficult for him to raise a reliable force, and by exceptionally bad autumn weather (even for England), which brought storms and so swelled the rivers that he could not easily cross into England. The southern rebels, who had planned their musters for 18 October at Exeter, Salisbury, Newbury (Berkshire) and various centres in the south-east, waited in vain for news of the duke's advance. Delay is usually destructive of rebel morale, discouraging the active and alarming the faint-hearted. When the news came, it was bad. Buckingham, deserted by his troops, was eventually betrayed in his hiding-place in Shropshire and was brought to the king at Salisbury. Denied any hearing by the furious Richard, he was executed on 2 November 1483 in Salisbury market-place. This, combined with the king's advance, effectively snuffed out the English rebellion. The rebels dispersed, if indeed many had not done so much earlier, and most of the leaders prudently took ship for France or Brittany. When Henry Tudor, his fleet hit by the autumn storms, eventually made a landfall in England (either at Poole in Dorset or Plymouth in Devon) it was to find the coast guarded and royal supporters waiting for him, and he too sailed back across the Channel.

Richard's easy and bloodless triumph could not conceal the fact that the rebellion of 1483 had serious consequences for his regime. In the first place, it greatly strengthened Henry Tudor's position as a contender for the English throne. He now had the backing in Brittany of a strong contingent of Yorkist dissidents, many of them experienced and able men who were afterwards to hold high positions in his government. He also had the sympathy of many who were left behind in England. Richard pardoned some of the rebels who chose not to flee abroad, but they could never be trusted again; and for security's sake some had to be arrested on the eve of Henry Tudor's second invasion. Secondly, the defection of so many southern gentry, the natural leaders of their county societies, created a problem of government for King Richard. With few reliable supporters left in England south and west of a line between London and Bristol, he was forced into ever-increasing dependence on his faithful northerners. The counties from Kent to Cornwall saw a virtual colonization of northern barons, knights and esquires, but the intrusion of such 'aliens' into the government and administration of these shires was deeply unpopular and much resented by the local populations. Men longed, it was said, for the return of their natural rulers, and groaned under the tyranny of the men from the north.

At the highest political level Richard's power-base, already dangerously slender, contracted still further. He had been heavily dependent from the start on the support of four overmighty subjects, Buckingham, John, Lord Howard, whom he had created Duke of Norfolk, Thomas, Lord Stanley, and Henry Percy, 4th Earl of Northumberland. Buckingham, his most powerful supporter, was now dead. The loyalty of Lord Stanley, now the third husband of Margaret Beaufort, was an uncertain quantity. Northumberland had probably resented being overshadowed in the north by Richard himself as Duke of Gloucester, and Richard's accession did not bring a restoration of the Percy dominance which he might have hoped for. In a letter written soon after Bosworth, he is fairly reliably reported as one of the magnates who gave a favourable response to Henry Tudor's agents, and certainly his ambiguous behaviour at Bosworth showed how unwise Richard had been to depend upon him. Dubious as these pillars of the regime were, Richard was in no position to destroy or replace them. Only John

The young Henry VII (*left*), with tomb effigies of his mother, Margaret Beaufort (*below left*), and his future wife, Elizabeth of York (*below*).

John Howard, Duke of Norfolk: a stained-glass picture, now destroyed, but once in Tendring Hall, Suffolk – birthplace of the duke.

Howard could be relied upon to serve Richard with the same unswerving loyalty as he had once given to his former master, Edward IV.

Naturally, Richard tried hard to broaden the basis of his support. He now had a huge fund of offices and lands at his disposal, forfeited from Buckingham and the rebels of 1483, and he at once began a massive distribution of patronage in the hope of buying committed support. These measures had some success, although too much of Richard's largesse went to the three great men and to his dependable northerners; and they might have been more successful still if only Richard had been allowed more time to consolidate his position. Richard was by no means the personification of evil which he was to become in the hands of hostile Tudor propagandists. He had charm, energy and ability, and he worked hard to win popularity. But it took time to live down the legacy of suspicion and mistrust generated by the violence of his usurpation. Even in that ruthless age, many men were appalled by what they clearly believed to have been his crime against the princes. The murder of innocent boys by the man whose special duty it was to protect them was thought to have a specially heinous quality. Had Henry Tudor's invasion been long delayed, its outcome might have been very different, but in 1485 Richard was still far from having won the confidence of his people in general.

Henry Tudor was certainly fortunate. In Brittany he narrowly managed to escape being captured and turned over to the English, and made good his escape to France. There the government, which was anxious to absorb Brittany into France, and feared that Richard III would support the Breton independence movement, decided to aid Henry's invasion. Supplied by France with money, ships and some 3,000 French troops, he set sail for Wales in August 1485 – but just in the nick of time, for French policy changed abruptly immediately after his departure. A month's delay, and the necessary French support might have been withdrawn. Richard III had long been expecting an invasion and had taken measures against it. His problem was that he could not know where Henry might descend. Fifteenth-century invaders had landed at a variety of places from west Wales, round the south and east coasts of England, to as far north as Northumberland. Unlike Edward IV, he does not seem to have relied for protection and early warning on naval patrols, perhaps because he was desperately short of money, but he had stationed his supporters at strategic points along the coast, and himself took up station at Nottingham, as a convenient point from which to march in any direction.

These defence arrangements were partially successful. Henry Tudor evidently feared to risk a descent on the south coast, and instead landed at Milford Haven in west Wales, where Jasper Tudor still had some support, on 7 August 1485. South Wales was closed against him by Richard's supporter, William Herbert, Earl of Huntingdon and son of the 1st Earl of Pembroke, who had married the king's bastard daughter, Katherine, and he was forced to march first north, and then east across mid-Wales, to enter England via Shrewsbury on 15 August. News of Henry's landing reached Richard III on 11 August, and he at once summoned his chief supporters to meet him with their men at Leicester. In the course of the next few days the two forces gradually converged until they met at Bosworth on 22 August.

It is important to realize that, although Richard had justifiable worries about the loyalty of some of his captains and their men, the forces at his command were still far greater than those of Henry Tudor. The invader had received the backing of the ambitious and quite powerful Welshman, Rhys ap Thomas, and of Sir Gilbert Talbot, an uncle of the young Earl of Shrewsbury, with some 500 men. Otherwise, no English nobleman or knight had openly declared for his cause. The hesitation of Thomas, Lord Stanley, and his brother, Sir William, who had almost certainly promised him their support, is to be explained by the fact that Richard held his son, George, as hostage for their good behaviour. None the less, Henry's position was scarcely less desperate than that of Edward IV in the early stages of his 1471 campaign, with the added disadvantage that, unlike Edward, he was now being challenged by the full power of a royal army led by the king in person. It is a sign of the effects on

Overleaf: rival kings fighting; from a manuscript of *c.* 1454. At Bosworth in 1485 Richard III and Henry Tudor came close to this type of personal combat.

the English nobility and gentry of thirty years of dynastic upheaval and political violence that, whatever their feelings about Richard, so few were prepared to risk life and fortune in a struggle for the throne, at least on behalf of an unknown like Henry Tudor. In the end, popular mistrust or resentment of Richard III had little to do with his overthrow. His undoing came from the treachery of two great men, Northumberland and Stanley. (The Battle of Bosworth itself is described in more detail in the next chapter.) The career of Richard III is the supreme object-lesson in the dangers to political security which came from the existence of overmighty subjects. It was as one such that he had been able to usurp the throne (during a minority) in 1483, and it was perhaps appropriate that his downfall came from the actions of two more, whom he himself had helped to aggrandize.

The final chapter of the civil war demonstrates how insecure was the position of any English monarch, so long as foreign powers were prepared to dabble in English domestic discords, so long as there was no reservoir of committed loyalty to the crown among nobility and gentry, and so long as everything depended on the outcome of a single battle. With the change of dynasty in England, two things changed in England's foreign situation. The first was the position of Ireland. Years before, in the attempt to secure for himself an independent power-base in Ireland, Duke Richard of York had encouraged the aspirations of the Anglo-Irish nobility to 'Home Rule'. When his son became king as Edward IV, after one abortive attempt to reassert English royal control, he allowed this situation to continue, and had no further trouble with Ireland. The Anglo-Irish ruled themselves, dominated by the great FitzGerald family, in the persons of Thomas and Gerald, 7th and 8th Earls of Kildare. To preserve this independence, which the new king might not wish to tolerate, the Anglo-Irish obviously had a vested interest in assisting any Yorkist efforts to recover the throne, and Ireland became a useful base for Yorkist pretenders.

The other change was in the position of Burgundy, or rather of the dowager-duchess, Margaret of York. Although not in control of official ducal policy, she had wealth and resources of her own, and soon proved herself a dedicated antagonist of the Tudor dynasty. Her court became a refuge for Yorkists, among them Francis, Viscount Lovell, who had been one of Richard III's closest friends and supporters, and later John de la Pole, Earl of Lincoln, whom Richard may have recognized as heir presumptive to the throne after the death from natural causes of his little son, Edward, Prince of Wales, in 1484. Duchess Margaret backed the cause of the first Yorkist pretender, Lambert Simnel, the ten-year-old son of an Oxford carpenter, who posed as Edward, Earl of Warwick, son of the Duke of Clarence. Unlikely as this imposture was – for the real Earl of Warwick was in the Tower and could be produced by Henry VII – it became a dangerous threat to Henry's throne because of the powerful interests involved. Duchess Margaret supplied ships and a strong force of German mercenary troops; Lincoln and Lovell lent their support; the Anglo-Irish crowned Lambert as Edward VI in Dublin on 24 May 1487, and added to his army a large number of brave but ill-trained Irishmen. The rebels landed in Lancashire on 4 June. Their hopes of attracting support in the city and county of York and in the north generally were disappointed, especially since the Stanleys remained loyal to the king. It was, therefore, essentially the German-Irish army which clashed with the royal forces at Stoke on 16 June 1487. Henry VII finally triumphed in a hard-fought battle, but it might easily have gone the other way. Again, as in 1485, it is remarkable how many noblemen and gentry avoided committing themselves to the struggle.

Lambert Simnel was not the last Yorkist impostor to challenge the Tudor throne, and other and more genuine Yorkist claimants could not resist the temptation to become involved in treasonable activity. Henry VII's lease on his royal property was far from secure. Indeed, the entire history of the Tudor regime was racked by conspiracy, plot, rebellion and dynastic uncertainty. But the Battle of Stoke was the last occasion on which the reigning king was required to take the field in person against a rival claimant to his throne, and, with it, the long chapter of English history when rivals to the throne confronted each other on the battlefield came to an end.

John de la Pole, Duke of Suffolk, and his wife, in Wingfield Church, Suffolk. His son, the Earl of Lincoln, had become Richard III's nearest male heir in 1484, and led the rebellion against Henry VII which ended with Lincoln's death at the Battle of Stoke in 1487.

ELIZABETHA · VXOR
HENRICI · VII ·

Elizabeth of York, daughter of Edward IV, and queen of Henry VII, holding the White Rose of York. Under Henry VII the roses were usually bi-coloured, Red for Lancaster and White for York, symbolizing the union of the two families.

Henry VII, a portrait by Michael Sittow, 1505.

Chapter Four

BATTLES AND BATTALIONS
THE MILITARY ASPECTS OF THE WAR

Shakespeare made the greater battles of the Wars of the Roses – Barnet and Bosworth, Towton and Tewkesbury – part of the folklore of English history. Particular battles and the clash of individual combatants certainly have their own dramatic interest, though students of military history in the more professional sense – that is, the evolution of strategy, tactics and logistics – have always found the Wars of the Roses a rather thorny and unrewarding subject. For this there are two main reasons.

The first revolves round the problem of evidence. The simple truth is that we know remarkably little about the fighting of the years 1455–87. No fifteenth-century Churchill, Montgomery or Eisenhower set out to describe the war. Still less did any fighting officer or private soldier (as John Page had in the remarkable poem which described the horrors of Henry V's siege of Rouen in 1417–18). Apart from the slender account of the campaigns of Edward IV in 1470–71, there is no such thing as an official history, certainly nothing to compare with the multi-volumed histories which nowadays serve the student of the First and Second World Wars. We do not even possess the lengthy paean of homage to a dying code of chivalry in which Froissart recounted (however misleadingly) the Anglo-French conflict of the fourteenth century. For only four of the thirteen battles of the Wars of the Roses (1st and 2nd St Albans, Barnet and Tewkesbury) do we have anything approaching an eyewitness account. Mostly, we depend on brief notices in chronicles and histories, many of them compiled years after the event, and usually written by men who were far away from the fighting. Such accounts as do exist often conflict on essential points of evidence. Consequently it is frequently hard to produce an acceptable narrative. Even for one of the major and decisive battles like Bosworth we remain ignorant of the precise sequence of events. There is also tremendous uncertainty about the numbers of men engaged in the fighting and about the casualty figures, a point more fully discussed below.

Opposite: the Battle of Barnet, 1471; from a French version of the official Yorkist chronicle of the campaign, *The Arrivall.*

Longbowmen confront crossbowmen at Crécy: the victors were not in doubt.

The second reason concerns the nature of the fighting itself. Most battles of the civil war were fought between armies which were of similar size, but even more important, of similar composition and without any decisive advantage in terms of tactics or firepower. To appreciate this point properly, it should be seen in a wider context. To the military historian, the main interest of the later Middle Ages lies in the steady rise in importance of armies composed of non-noble soldiers, always infantrymen, as compared with the mounted cavalry, often noblemen, which had dominated the battlefields of Europe in the twelfth and thirteenth centuries. As early as 1302 the Battle of Courtrai demonstrated the superiority of disciplined pikemen from the Flemish towns over the heavy cavalry of France. Twelve years later, at Bannockburn, the mounted English nobility plunged to disaster against the embattled pikes of the Scots infantry. This same lesson was to be taught over and over again, by English archers in the Hundred Years War, by Swiss pikemen against the Habsburgs and the Burgundians, by Bohemian gunners – arquebusiers and hackbuteers – in the Hussite Wars of the early fifteenth century; and, towards the end of the century, by the splendid infantry of Castile, which made its first significant appearance in the conquest of Granada (1482–89), and was later to dominate the battlefields of sixteenth-century Europe.

In the long-drawn-out wars with France, whence the English derived their military experience and expertise, their decisive superiority lay in the firepower and effectiveness of their long-bowmen. If their arrows lacked the weight and penetration of those of the Genoese crossbowmen employed by the French, the English archers could shoot ten to twelve arrows a minute against the crossbowmen's two, over an effective range of about 165 yards. They could rain a deadly shower of shafts on advancing cavalry, and were particularly lethal against unprotected horses. To counter this threat, the French switched from the chain-mail of earlier times (which could be penetrated by an arrow) to elaborate and very expensive plate-armour, and began experimenting with armouring their horses. The massive weight of equipment which resulted led them either to abandon horse-armour, in order to preserve mobility, or to dismount and fight on foot: and a man weighed down by as much as 110 lb of arms and armour had but a limited endurance, especially in hot weather. But the English were successful only so long as they had leisure to take up a strong defensive position and

Armour of the mounted cavalryman, German, c. 1475. Most armour worn by persons of rank during the Wars of the Roses was manufactured abroad.

protect their archers with extensive lines of stakes and pikes, and so long as the French continued to attack them impetuously in such positions. When caught on the move, or when they themselves attacked, they lost all advantage and suffered defeat in their turn.

In the course of the later Middle Ages the steady development of artillery introduced an entirely new weapon to European warfare. The larger cannon – and by 1460 a bombard such as *Mons Meg*, now at Edinburgh Castle, weighed over 14,000 lb and had a calibre of more than 20 inches – were used mainly for siege warfare. Their sheer weight and lack of mobility made them unsuitable for use on the battlefield, but in the fifteenth century the French in particular pioneered the development of much lighter and more mobile field-guns, which could be carried along in the wake of a marching army. The first battle to be decided by the use of artillery was the last engagement of the Hundred Years War: at Castillon in 1453, when the English under John Talbot, Earl of Shrewsbury, made the fatal decision to attack a strong French position protected by cannon, and were cut to pieces for their pains. English experience on the Continent probably explains the rapid development of artillery in England, and, as we shall see, an artillery train became a regular part of an army's equipment. Cannon were to be used in all the major engagements of the Wars of the Roses. By contrast, hand-guns, which were something of a German speciality, attracted little favour among Englishmen, who rightly believed in the superiority of their native longbow over weapons which were still inefficient, took a long time to reload, and were vulnerable to rain and damp. Consequently, hand-guns were almost unknown in the Wars of the Roses.

When Englishman fought Englishman at home, neither side possessed any of the technical advantages we have described. Each army usually had its complement of cavalry, of archers, of foot-soldiers equipped with spear, pike and halberd, and a contingent of cannon. The presence of archers on both sides, and the consequent threat to horses, often compelled commanders to adopt the French technique of making their cavalry dismount. Instead they fought on foot as heavy infantry, armed with swords and battle-axes, or with maces and flails – great spiked balls of iron attached to a staff by a long chain. These latter weapons were the answer to the increasingly sophisticated fluted armour, much of it imported from Italy, which was developed during the fifteenth century. Armour of this kind could often deflect arrow, sword or spear: the mace or flail could crush both the armour and the man within it by sheer weight of impact. Very heavily armoured men could not, however, fight on foot for long without becoming exhausted, and this is one reason why most battles of the civil war rarely lasted for more than two or three hours. The bloody engagement at Towton in 1461 is quite exceptional in that it lasted from dawn until dusk on a March day.

The armoured soldier – 'How a man shall be armed at his ease when he shall fight on foot', *c.* 1480 *(left)*; in close combat, *c.* 1485–90 *(below left)*; and in full Italian armour, *c.* 1450 *(below right)*.

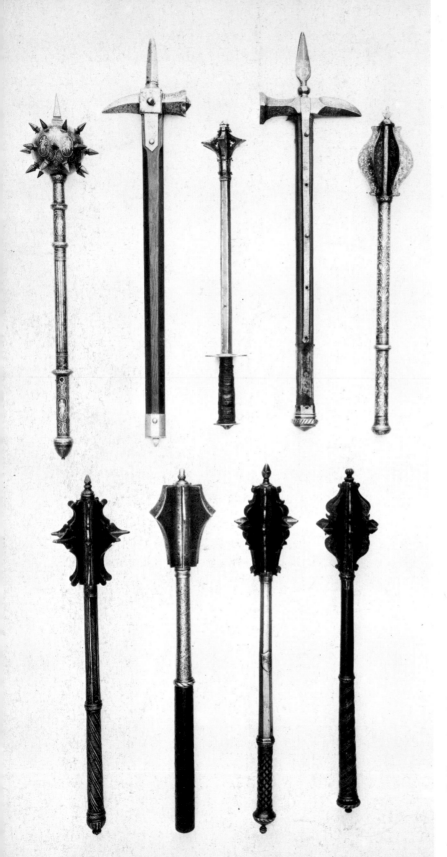

Left: the weapons of the close-combat mellay, used by men of rank: designed to crush rather than to pierce the opponent's armour. Compare the spears and halberds of the rank-and-file infantry opposite.

Equally the contingents of archers and of guns on both sides tended to cancel each other out. Given a favourable opportunity (as at Towton or Tewkesbury), they could be used to draw the enemy from his position, but as soon as hand-to-hand fighting was joined, the relatively lightly armoured archer, usually protected only by a steel cap or sallet and a brigandine or steel jerkin which covered his trunk, was at a severe disadvantage compared with a man encased in plate-armour carrying far heavier weapons. They were also vulnerable to the fire of their enemy counterparts. Since they were no longer confronted by the suicidal cavalry charges which they had faced in France, their longbow ceased to be the decisive weapon it had been abroad. Battles often began with an exchange of fire from bows and guns, but thereafter neither weapon exercised much influence on the final outcome, and it is a striking fact that many battles were won by the attacking side, in sharp contrast to the defensive victories of the English during the Hundred Years War.

Consequently, nearly all the battles of the civil war, though not without their features of individual interest, were essentially slugging-matches: their main common element was the hand-to-hand mellay, fought on foot, and involving all ranks from the expensively armed nobleman down to the common soldier. In these conditions, much depended on the quality, experience and morale of the individual soldier. There was a great deal of difference between the retainers and men-at-arms who served in the immediate retinues of the nobility and wealthier knights – men bred and trained in the profession of arms, and generally much better equipped – and the local levies of yeomen, farm-workers and artisans raised from the countryside who made up the bulk of the armies. This very point was made by one of the very few contemporary chroniclers who had actual experience of battle. He was a London citizen who fought as a foot-soldier under the Earl of Warwick at 2nd St Albans against Queen Margaret's northern army. Interestingly enough, he provides early testimony for the infantryman's traditional contempt for the easy life of the cavalry. 'As for spearmen [he says] they be good to ride before the footmen and eat and drink up their victuals, and many such pretty things they do, hold me excused though I say the best, for in the footmen is all the trust.' But he also observed that the battle-winning element in the queen's victorious army was the professional men-at-arms in the service of their lords: 'The substance that got the field were household men and fee'd men. I ween there were not a 5,000 men that fought in the queen's party, for the most part of the northern men [that is, the country levies] fled away, and some were taken and spoiled out of their harness by the way as they fled.'

It may well be that one of the reasons for Edward IV's victory at Tewkesbury was the presence in his army of a much larger proportion of lords and their retainers as compared with the less professional levies assembled from the west country by the Lancastrian leaders.

Professional soldiers were naturally better trained and disciplined, and were likely to be much steadier in a crisis. This contrast became clear in the closely contested Battle of Stoke in 1487, one of the two battles of the war where, as we have seen, foreign troops played an important part (Bosworth was the other). Here the royal army under Henry VII, with the Earl of Oxford and Lord Strange in support, confronted a mixed force under the rebel leader, the Earl of Lincoln. Many of the rebels were half-naked Irish levies, but the core of Lincoln's army was a contingent of 2,000 tough German mercenaries under an experienced captain named Schwarz, supplied and paid for by Duchess Margaret of Burgundy. In the initial rebel attack on the royal vanguard under Oxford, the Irish fought bravely and well, but, as resistance stiffened and more royalist troops came up in support, they broke and fled. On the other hand, the Germans stood their ground, although now heavily outnumbered, and eventually were cut down almost to a man. Probably they formed a large part of the 4,000 casualties which the rebels are said – no doubt with exaggeration – to have suffered.

What then of the commanders? Given the similar composition of the rival armies, and the lack of any decisive advantage except in sheer weight in numbers, the battles of the civil war offered little

Most battles of the period developed into hard-fought, hand-to-hand mellays.

scope for imaginative or resourceful generalship. The Wars of the
Roses did not, indeed could not, in the circumstances, produce any
medieval Marlborough or Napoleon. A nearer comparison might
be with the German tank-generals of the Second World War, a
Guderian or a Rommel, who led their troops into battle from the
apex of the formation. For personal bravery and prowess were
essential requisites in a successful fifteenth-century commander.
Kings, princes and noblemen were expected to lead their men into
the fighting and inspire them by their own personal example.
Nearly all of them did, with the conspicuous exception of the feeble
Henry VI, who was more at home with a crucifix than a sword. He
was reported to have been wounded in the neck at 1st St Albans
while standing alone, apparently ineffectual, beside his overturned
and unattended royal standard. Even before the fighting was over
he was conveyed to St Albans Abbey for safety on the orders of
the Duke of York. He seems to have been little more than a passive
spectator at the five battles where he was, rather remotely, present,
and there is no record of his having wielded anything more lethal
than a prayer-book. His military and probably mental feebleness is
highlighted by the frequency with which he was taken prisoner (no
less than three times), since he apparently lacked the wit or the
energy to escape from a losing field. At last, in 1464 at Hexham, his
friends took the precaution of placing him in Bywell Castle, some
miles away from the fighting, from where, an ageing Prince Charlie,
he was safely spirited away to a hiding-place in the Pennines, leaving
his crown behind.

Otherwise, army commanders, and their lieutenants who commanded the principal divisions (or 'battles' as they were called), were to be found in the thick of the fighting. Their great banners carried beside them by a trusted standard-bearer often formed the only visible rallying-point amid the confusion of a mellay. Even if they were flanked and protected by their bodyguards of household men, the personal risks were high, for they were obviously a prime target of enemy attacks. Andrew Trollope, a seasoned professional veteran of the French wars, was knighted for his prowess after 2nd St Albans by the youthful Lancastrian Prince of Wales: 'My lord [he said] I have not deserved it, for I slew but fifteen men; for I stood still in one place, and they came unto me, but they bide still with me.' The official Yorkist chronicle of the 1471 campaign, known as *The Arrivall of King Edward IV*, has left us a spirited account of the king's personal prowess at the Battle of Barnet:

> the king, trusting verily in God's help, our blessed Lady's and St George . . . with the faithful, well-beloved and mighty assistance of his fellowship [i.e. his household men] that in great number dissevered not from his person, and were as well assured unto him as to them was possible . . . he manly, vigorously and valiantly assailed them [the enemy] in the midst of the strongest of their battle, where he, with great violence, beat and bore down before him all that stood in his way, and then turned to the range, first on that one hand, and then on that other hand, so beat and bear them down that nothing might stand in the sight of him and that well-assured fellowship that attended truly upon him.

Edward survived to win the day, but many commanders involved in close combat did not. Their very position at the centre of the fighting made them vulnerable both to death and to capture as the fighting ended. There was a very heavy casualty rate among the leaders of high rank. Three Dukes of Somerset died in battle or were taken prisoner and executed immediately afterwards. Two Earls of Northumberland were slain, one at 1st St Albans, one at Towton. An Earl of Devon died at Towton, another at Tewkesbury. Warwick and Montagu were killed at Barnet, the Lancastrian Prince of Wales at Tewkesbury, King Richard III and the Duke of Norfolk at Bosworth, the Earl of Lincoln at Stoke. Excluding kings and princes, twelve noblemen died in the fighting between 1459 and 1461, and six more were executed. In the period 1469–71 ten were killed and seven executed. Five died in 1483–85, and two more at Stoke in 1487.

This also explains why several battles were decided by the deaths of leading captains. Men laid down their arms and refused to fight further (as at 1st St Albans) when their leader fell and his banner no longer streamed above their divisions. This, too, is why Richard III decided upon his fatal charge at Bosworth in the hope of killing his rival Henry Tudor. Yet it is also obvious that when the principal commander was himself directly involved in the thick of the fighting, there was little scope for tactical manœuvre or intelligent generalship. Once his troops had been engaged, the issue depended

t ouraque aeste battaille
ansy aduenu le roy setrav
en la ville de tabliebni
en laqlle lui la venie

Richard Neville
Earl of Warwick
1449 — 1471.

The bear, badge of Richard Nevill, Earl of Warwick: a notable failure as a general.

on factors beyond his control – the morale of the troops, good fortune, treachery or the outcome of close hand-to-hand fighting. Occasionally a commander could exploit a particular advantage – of weather, position or the enemy's ignorance. At Towton in 1461, we are told, William, Lord Fauconberg, commanding a division on the Yorkist side, conducted an effective deception against the Lancastrians. He was advancing towards the enemy, who were blinded by the strong wind driving snow into their faces. He therefore ordered his archers, now within extreme range, to fire a single volley and then withdraw. In response, the unsighted Lancastrians fired off volley after volley until their quivers were drained. The Yorkists then collected the discharged arrows and continued their attack. Yet even this device did not prevent the battle turning into a bloody hand-to-hand engagement, which was partially decided by the arrival from the Yorkist rear of fresh forces from the Duke of Norfolk's command.

One general, the Earl of Warwick, who was very defensively minded and also notably unsuccessful, devoted much time and effort to counter-measures against the expected Lancastrian attack at 2nd St Albans. They are described by William Gregory, the London chronicler who fought with Warwick. He was clearly impressed by their ingenuity and depressed by their ineffectiveness against a surprise attack. Warwick's gunners, he tells us, were equipped with a sort of primitive grapeshot, a mixture of pellets of lead and huge arrows, an ell (45 inches) in length, with six feathers, three in the middle and three at the rear end, with a great head of iron, 'and wild

Opposite: the battle over, retribution follows: the execution of the Duke of Somerset after Tewkesbury, 1471.

fire withal'. In front of Warwick's line his men had spread 'nets made of great cords of three fathoms [18 feet] of length and 4 feet broad, like to a hay [rabbit net], and at every second knot there was a nail standing upright, [so] that there could no man pass over it by likelihood but he should be hurt'. Warwick also seems to have made use of the caltrap, a sort of star-fish made of steel spikes so arranged that in whatever position it lay one spike always projected upwards. When thickly laid caltraps offered an obvious and nasty threat to charging horses and men. Among Warwick's other devices were a number of pavises – a kind of sandwich-board to protect an archer – which contained windows from which a man could shoot: these were thickly covered with large nails, so that when the archer had exhausted his arrows, he could lay it flat to ward off the enemy with yet another prickly hazard. In practice, none of this hardware achieved any result, for, misled by their scouts, Warwick's men were taken by surprise and overrun before they could bring their elaborate firepower to bear upon the enemy.

King Edward IV, victorious in four engagements and defeated in none, was the most consistently successful commander to emerge from the Wars of the Roses. In a later age, he might have made an excellent strategist, for he appreciated the importance of speed of movement, the seizure of vital places and the psychological advantages of attack given the right circumstances. These qualities were best displayed during the fast-moving six-week campaign of 1471, which proved to be very much his personal triumph. In this brief spell he was able to march from Yorkshire to defeat Warwick and the Nevills at Barnet, to take control of London, and, by an extraordinarily rapid operation, to intercept and defeat Queen Margaret's troops at Tewkesbury before the Lancastrian forces could achieve their full strength. If, however, his enemies had come at him together instead of singly the story might have been a very different one, as Polydore Vergil very properly pointed out.

Something of Edward's quality as a commander emerges from the immediately contemporary official narrative of the campaign written by one of his supporters, known as *The Arrivall of King Edward IV*. Despite a certain partisan bias, this account possesses the great advantage of sharp and vivid reporting by someone who was an eye-witness of the events he describes. The author tells in some detail how Edward outmanoeuvred and out-generalled the hesitant Earl of Warwick on his march south from Yorkshire to take control once more of London. Warwick, circumvented at Coventry through his own timidity, followed Edward south, believing himself still secure either because London would keep the king out, 'which failed', or because 'in case he were received in, he should there have kept and observed the solemnity of Easter, and, if he so did, he [Warwick] thought suddenly to come upon him, take him, and destroy him'. But Edward was not to be deceived, and on the evening before Easter Sunday (13 April 1471) he marched out of

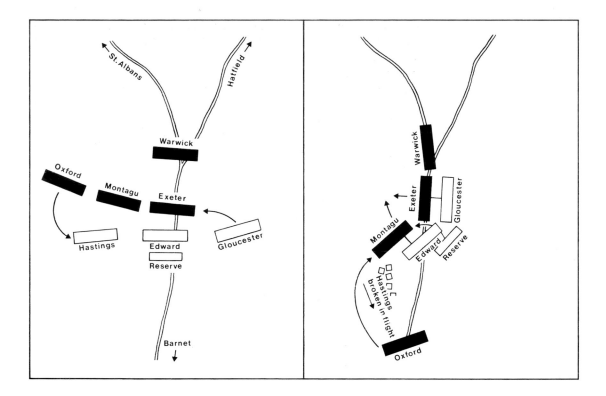

London with his army. Ten miles from London at Barnet his scouts met those of Warwick and chased them out of the town, until they discovered Warwick in position 'by a hedge-side' half a mile further north. Hearing this, Edward forced his men forward in the growing darkness, and they took up a position closer to Warwick's forces than they had supposed and not in direct alignment with them 'but somewhat aside-hand'. Both parties, says *The Arrivall*, had guns and ordnance, but there were many more on the earl's side. Hoping to incommode Edward's men, Warwick's guns kept up a steady fire during the night, but because the armies were so close they overshot; and Edward had taken the precaution – a sign of a good general – of enforcing silence on his troops, and backed this up, in order to deceive the enemy as to his position, by restricting the fire of his own cannon.

The early morning of Easter Sunday saw both armies veiled in a thick mist. Nevertheless, confident that Warwick's men would be taken by surprise, Edward launched his men forward even before full light 'betwixt four and five of the clock'. 'He committed his cause and quarrel to Almighty God, advanced banners, did blow up trumpets, and set upon them first with shot, and, then and soon, they joined and came to hand-strokes.' Yet it was not Edward's fierce surprise attack which was to decide the day. As the armies became locked in conflict, the fact that they were not lined up directly opposite each other began to tell. On Edward's left Hastings' 'battle'

The developing scene at the Battle of Barnet, 1471: the opposing forces at dawn (*left*) and towards the end of the battle (*right*).

or division was soon overlapped by the Lancastrian right under John de Vere, Earl of Oxford. The Yorkists broke and fled, with Oxford's men in headlong and uncontrollable pursuit. Fortunately for the morale of the other Yorkist divisions, the mist concealed this disaster from them, and they fought on bravely.

At the other end of the line, Gloucester's division on Edward's right pressed hard on the Lancastrian left under Exeter and this caused the entire battle-line to swivel until it lay at right angles to its original position. Consequently, when some 800 men of Oxford's division had been with difficulty regrouped and brought back to the battle, they were first sighted by their own side, who, in the mist, mistook their De Vere livery badge of the 'star with streams' for the Yorkist 'sun with streams' (the rising sun). The Lancastrians opened fire on Oxford's men who broke and fled, crying treason, which demoralized their fellows. Meanwhile, Montagu in the Lancastrian centre had been killed, and, fearing that the battle was turning against him, Warwick tried to escape on horseback (he had been fighting on foot), only to be cut down and killed as he galloped away towards Barnet Wood. According to this version (by the contemporary chronicler, John Warkworth), the mistake with Oxford's men was the decisive factor. However, the official version in *The Arrivall*, which does not mention this story, piously emphasizes instead the steadiness of the Yorkist centre and in particular the prowess of King Edward and his household men. Either way generalship had little to do with the outcome.

No sooner had the victorious Yorkists returned to London than Edward learned that Queen Margaret and the Prince of Wales had landed at Weymouth on the very day of Barnet. She was soon joined by old-guard Lancastrians like Somerset and Devon, and together they departed for Exeter to raise troops in the west country. Edward showed a keen appreciation of the need to confront her as soon as possible, and in particular to intercept her before she could join forces with the Welsh Lancastrians or reach the traditional areas of Lancastrian loyalty in Cheshire and the north Midlands. Raising fresh troops, collecting his artillery train, and sending spies westwards to divine her movements, he planned to meet her, if she were aiming for London, as far from the capital as possible to prevent her gathering more troops as she advanced. Alternatively, if she meant to march north, he must deny her the important Severn crossings. He correctly interpreted Lancastrian troop-movements in south Somerset as being no more than a feint, and himself set off towards Bristol to check the queen's progress. He arrived at Chipping Sodbury in Gloucestershire too late to prevent the city of Bristol providing the queen's army with men, money and artillery, and did not immediately discover that her forces were now pushing hard through the Vale of Berkeley towards Gloucester. Sending an urgent message to his constable there, Sir Richard Beauchamp, to close the city gates against the queen and deny her the use of the Severn

Opposite: the cipher of Margaret of Anjou on an angel in the roof of the hall at Queens' College, Cambridge. Margaret was an early patroness of the college, which was founded in 1448.

bridge, Edward hurled his forces in pursuit. All the next day, 3 May, the two armies moved in parallel, the Lancastrians in the 'foul country' of the Severn Vale, the Yorkists high up on the Cotswold escarpment. It was a very hot day, and Edward's men suffered agonies of thirst, for the few streams which lay on their route were fouled and muddied by horses and gun-carriages. Nevertheless, he urged his men on relentlessly and eventually arrived near Tewkesbury – after a monstrous march of 35 miles – to find the Lancastrians encamped near by. He had succeeded in his objective. It was too late in the day, and the queen's forces were too weary after their own long march, for them to attempt a crossing of the Severn by the ford at Tewkesbury that night. They now had no choice but to fight, for they could not cross with Edward's powerful army so close in their rear.

Early the following day Edward advanced with all his customary boldness. The Lancastrians had taken up a strong position on a low ridge with the town at their backs, looking down over a difficult stretch of ground, full of deep lanes, dykes, hedges, trees and bushes – far from ideal territory to deploy and manoeuvre a large army. Before committing himself to the attack, Edward had intelligently tried to achieve an element of surprise by concealing a force of 200 cavalry amid the trees of Tewkesbury Park near by, with orders to charge at their discretion. The battle began when the Yorkist vanguard, commanded by the Duke of Gloucester, opened fire with cannon and arrows on Somerset's men on the Lancastrian right. Goaded by this fire, or because he hoped to strike the Yorkists before they were fully deployed, Somerset now ordered his men to attack Gloucester under cover of the trees and lanes. His decision to abandon his good defensive position proved, however, to be a fatal move, for his forces were soon squeezed between the hammer of Gloucester's division and the anvil of the king's 'battle' in the Yorkist centre. In the usual hard hand-to-hand fighting Somerset's forces were gradually pressed back up the hill, and were then suddenly assailed by the 200 spears charging from the wood near by. They broke and fled.

Edward immediately pressed home his advantage, and his troops fell upon the Lancastrian centre under Edward, Prince of Wales, which was routed in its turn and was soon in full flight. Even then, to judge from the number of noble casualties, bitter fighting continued, until eventually the Lancastrian left was overpowered, and the battle became a murderous rout as the fugitives were cut down by the Yorkist cavalry in what later came to be known as 'Bloody Meadow'. It is hard to see that, apart from his use of the 200 spears, this victory represents any great triumph of generalship on Edward's part. It has been suggested that Edward's opening fire against Somerset's 'battle' was a deliberate tactical move intended to lure the enemy from their position, so that he could then intrude his own division into the gap, but this remains a mere surmise for which

Opposite: the Battle of Tewkesbury, 1471.

Dxés touttes ces choses amfy
advenues le sezieme sour du
dit mois le soy eut nouuelles
que marguerite soy disant soy

there is no direct evidence. It is equally possible that Somerset's attack was aimed at catching the Yorkists in difficult ground, and had he been supported by the other Lancastrian divisions, it might have succeeded. On the other hand, if they had all held their position, and thus forced the royal army to fight uphill into the teeth of the Lancastrian archers, the result might have been different. As it was, Somerset's advance enabled Edward to destroy the Lancastrian divisions piecemeal.

Throughout his campaign of 1471 Edward was attended by good fortune. He might have been destroyed in its early stages, when his forces were still puny and he was marching through a hostile countryside, had not the Earl of Northumberland kept his men at home, and prevented them from attacking Edward. Again the king might have been checked and defeated on his southward march if Warwick had been less timorous and there had been more co-ordination between him and the Lancastrian leaders. He was most fortunate of all in the fact that the landing of Queen Margaret was delayed by bad weather until after Warwick and Montagu had been overwhelmed at Barnet. Again, Fauconberg's dangerous rising in Kent, and his subsequent attack on London, did not develop until Edward had settled his accounts at Tewkesbury, and the news of his victory there helped not only to disperse the Kentish rebels but also to discourage would-be Nevill-Lancastrian rebels in the north of England. But Edward should not be shorn of too much of his military glory. Throughout the campaign he had acted with remarkable speed and decision, and, above all, he possessed a bold confidence in his own destiny and a capacity to inspire his men – and men will often fight well, even against odds, for a commander with a victorious reputation.

If Edward IV's military reputation has been somewhat exaggerated, that of his brother, Richard of Gloucester, has been even more inflated. Richard was fond of presenting himself in a martial image – it was he who incorporated the College of Arms in 1484 – but in fact his military experience was limited. His experience of battle was confined to serving as commander of a division at Barnet and Tewkesbury, where he seems to have acquitted himself well enough. His only independent command was during the English invasion of Scotland in 1482. This was a largely bloodless affair, for the Scots were too divided and demoralized to offer much resistance, and were only too anxious to negotiate with a vastly superior English army. The only outcome of an inconclusive and expensive military promenade was the recapture of the great border stronghold of Berwick-upon-Tweed, which Queen Margaret of Anjou had surrendered to the Scots twenty years before as the price of their assistance. When Richard came to the fatal field of Bosworth on 22 August 1485, it was, in fact, the first time he had been in overall command of an army in pitched battle. His forces, which included a number of noblemen and powerful contingents of tough northerners,

Opposite: Fauconberg's attack on London, 1471: the only assault on a walled town during the period of the civil war.

128

Iorc̃ le bastard de faucquemier
ctbe ct ſes compliceſ afrandc
violence le trezieme ct qua
touerme ſour dudit moiſ aſ
ſaillirent la cite de laudret auec traut

RICARDVS · III · ANG · REX

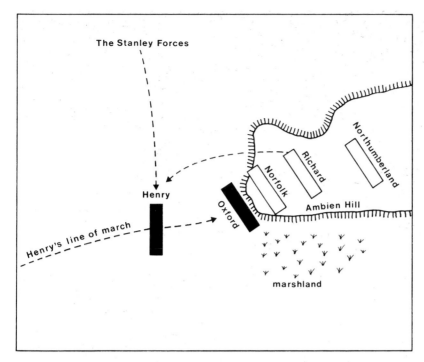

The Stanley Forces

Northumberland

Richard

Norfolk

Henry

Oxford

Ambien Hill

Henry's line of march

marshland

Richard III (*opposite*), defeated and killed at Bosworth, 1485 (*left*), the forces deployed in the battle.

were very much more formidable than the mixed force of French and Welsh levies which was all Henry Tudor could command. In a straight fight he should have carried the day with ease. But this was one of the battles where treachery prevailed over the big battalions.

There have been as many different accounts of Bosworth as there have been historians, and even today it is hard to produce a reconstruction of the battle which will command general acceptance. Richard's army was drawn up on a slight eminence known as Ambien Hill, the southern and eastern flanks of which were protected by an extensive area of marshland. The core of the royal army, archers, pikemen and gunners – the guns being chained together to prevent their being overridden – was aligned on the edge of the hill facing east, under the command of John Howard, Duke of Norfolk; the centre 'battle', mainly cavalry, lay behind with the king himself; and the Earl of Northumberland's large division, whose loyalty was dubious, was placed in the rearward. Somewhat to the north of Ambien Hill, on Richard's right, lay a large force of men under Sir William Stanley, and probably a smaller body commanded by Thomas, Lord Stanley. Neither of these had as yet committed themselves to either side, and they lay like an ominous thundercloud on the flank of the main engagement. If they did not support Henry Tudor, he faced almost certain annihilation, but in the circumstances he had little choice but to attack. To engage the royal army, Henry's army had to skirt the marsh and deploy in line of battle beneath Norfolk's men on the slope above. The main 'battle' of Henry's

Overleaf: the charge of the Yorkist knights at Bosworth; from a diorama in the Bosworth Museum.

army was commanded by the most experienced soldier on his side, John de Vere, Earl of Oxford. As the earl's men approached, they came under fire from Norfolk's guns and archers, and then, in the hope of catching them before their deployment was complete, Norfolk attacked, and the usual fierce hand-to-hand fighting took place (in which Norfolk may have been killed). The struggle was indecisive, and Norfolk's men temporarily drew back.

It was probably at this point that Henry decided on a direct appeal to the Stanleys. Accompanied only by his own personal bodyguard, he set off towards Sir William Stanley's position. This move was observed by the king, who had had no success in getting Northumberland to engage, and was now fearful of the outcome if Stanley became committed. He therefore launched himself and the main body of his cavalry, perhaps 1,000 strong, down the hill in the hope of cutting off Henry Tudor and destroying him before he could make contact with the Stanleys. This may have been an overly impetuous move on Richard's part, but was probably logical in his circumstances: the longer the battle lasted without moving decisively in his favour, the greater the risk of desertions from his side. If he could finish off Henry Tudor, then probably the issue of the day was decided in his favour. His charge came close to success, but not close enough. Sir William Brandon, Henry's standard-bearer, was killed on the point of Richard's lance, and close hand-to-hand fighting followed. Richard was unhorsed, but continued to defend himself valiantly on foot, and refused the offer of another horse to flee the field. The hard struggle round the two leaders was also a moment of truth for Sir William Stanley. If he did not now commit his troops on Henry's side, and Richard won the day, his future was gloomy. His sudden attack on the flank of the royalist cavalry would probably have proved decisive in itself, but even more decisive was the death of King Richard in the struggle round the banners. With their leader dead, Richard's men had little reason to continue the fighting. On the evidence of a battle in which questions of loyalty and disloyalty were so much more important than purely military considerations, it is quite impossible to judge Richard III's qualities as a general. His military ability remains an open question, but his courage at least is not in doubt.

How large were the armies which fought in these battles? This is a vexed and vexing problem. For the most part our information comes from statements made by contemporary chroniclers. At best these might be called (in a modern jargon-term) 'guesstimates', provided by men far removed in time and place from the events they were describing, who had little knowledge of war and were prone to exaggeration, as medieval people often were. To describe a large force, take the number you first thought of, double it and add a few for the pot: some such crude formula seems to have been the basis for the chroniclers' grievously exaggerated figures. Take, for instance, the London chronicle compiled by William Gregory,

Opposite: cavalry advancing at Bosworth; from the Bosworth Museum diorama.

whose author at least fought in a battle, which was more than most contemporary writers could claim. At 2nd St Albans, where he was present, he tells us that the Yorkist army numbered 100,000 men. At Towton, where he was not, he puts the Yorkist force at 200,000 men. Since everyone is agreed that the Lancastrians at Towton were much more numerous, we end with a figure of some half a million men engaged on both sides. This was at a time when the total population of England did not exceed two and a half million, and of these about 25 per cent at the very most – about 600,000 – were men of fighting age. According to Gregory, therefore, almost every adult male in England was engaged at Towton. Such figures beggar belief, and it is for this reason that almost all modern historians have been inclined to reduce most drastically the estimates of contemporaries for the numbers engaged.

It is true that many of the greater magnates could raise very substantial forces, given time and a cause which commanded the loyalty of their followers. In the early sixteenth century one of the Earl of Northumberland's bailiffs calculated that his master could raise no less than 11,241 men from his northern estates for service against the Scots. Such figures are by no means incredible in the light of a contract of 1448, when a Westmorland esquire, Walter Strickland of Sizergh Castle, undertook to supply the Earl of Salisbury with the service of 290 armed men; and Salisbury, like Northumberland, probably had about 40 or 50 men like Strickland on his payroll at any one time. The north of England, however, was noted as a reservoir of fighting men, even if its population was thinner than that of the Midlands and the south, and it was after all a frontier province organized for war against the Scots. But if the English magnates generally had been able to raise forces on this scale, then the numbers of men involved in the fighting would have been very large indeed. At Towton, for example, no less than four dukes, four earls and twenty barons took part. In practice, it seems they did not. In 1471 William, Lord Hastings, one of the most influential men in the Midlands, was able to raise 3,000 men on behalf of King Edward. This fits in well with the figure of 3,000 men which, according to a chronicler's estimate, Sir William Stanley was able to produce at Bosworth. In 1484 John Howard, Duke of Norfolk, by then among the most powerful men in the realm, counted on producing more than 1,000 men from his East Anglian estates alone.

What restricted the size of the armies was the unwillingness of the rank-and-file to serve far from home or for long periods. The great bulk of the men who fought in the civil war were not professional soldiers, but local levies. We know the names and occupations of 700 men who were indicted for their share in the 'Battle' of Heworth near York in 1453 (part of the private war between the Percies and the Nevills). No less than 94 per cent of these came from Yorkshire. The great majority were yeomen or tenant-farmers, with a stiffening of knights and gentry, and a considerable sprinkling of artisans and tradesmen from the city of York. There was also a significant handful of priests and chaplains. Similarly, in 1470, when Lord FitzHugh sought mercy from Edward IV for raising rebellion against him, the pardon named 185 of his supporters – and it is worth noticing that this small number apparently constituted a 'rebellion'. The vast majority were yeomen, the rest mainly gentlemen (technically a rank below knight and esquire) or members of FitzHugh's own family. Almost without exception they came from his north Yorkshire estate of Ravensworth or its immediate vicinity. Such men, who were not paid for their services, could rarely be counted upon to march long distances from their homelands, and there were also difficulties in feeding and supplying them while living 'off the land'. The men of Devon and Cornwall, for example, had little interest in events in the north. When in 1497 Henry VII proposed merely to tax them in order to resist a Scots invasion, he produced a serious insurrection in the far south-west. In this sense, the Wars of the Roses were essentially – but with important exceptions like Towton, St Albans and Bosworth – a series of local conflicts. By contrast with the Great Civil War in England in the seventeenth century, there were no such things as 'national' armies, based upon deep divisions of religious belief or political opinion. This was not, for the most part, a conflict fought upon issues of principle (such as the relative authority of king and Parliament, so much a theme of the Civil War of the seventeenth century). It was rather the product of a strongly hierarchical society, where the ties of dependence and loyalty spread downwards as from the apex of a pyramid – king to magnate to gentry, and so to their varied and numerous dependents: and such ties were usually regional or local in character.

The tomb of Sir Nicholas Fitzherbert (1473), Yorkist 'sunbursts' round his collar.

Seal of Edward IV.

What largely determined the size of the armies engaged was the importance of the occasion and the numbers of nobles involved. When both sides felt a vital point had been reached, and when both had been given time to recruit all their available supporters, then, by the standards of the day, very large numbers of men might be put into the field. This was particularly true when rivals for the throne clashed in the field. At Towton it was of vital importance for Henry VI and his queen to defeat the new king, Edward IV, before he could win general acceptance, and no less important for him to overwhelm the still active Lancastrians in order to gain recognition. As a result there was an unparalleled turn-out of nobility (some 75 per cent of the surviving adult peerage) and gentry, together with their followers, and it is not unlikely that as many as 50,000 men were involved. Some modern writers would go as high as 75,000. Probably these numbers were never matched again, for in 1471, as we have seen, Edward IV fought his two main groups of enemies separately; by the time of Bosworth the nobility were becoming increasingly reluctant to become involved and the number of barons present in 1485 was not nearly so high as it had been in 1461. At Barnet Edward IV is reliably said to have had about 9,000 men under his command, while Warwick's forces are generally agreed to have been very much larger – the same sources say 20,000 to 30,000, but

15,000 is a more likely estimate, making 24,000 in all. For Tewkesbury we have no reliable figures at all. It is probable that the armies were more evenly matched than at Barnet, perhaps with Edward having the advantage, but the total numbers engaged were in all probability not much higher than they had been at Barnet.

By 1485 the forces were smaller still. Henry Tudor is said to have had about 5,000 men in his army; Sir William Stanley commanded a further 3,000; and Polydore Vergil (who was writing twenty years after the event) tells us that the king's army was more than twice as large as Henry's. So perhaps some 20,000 to 25,000 men were engaged in all. At Stoke in 1487 the numbers were about the same. The rebels under Lincoln mustered some 9,000 men; the Stanleys (again according to Polydore) provided Henry with some 6,000; and their contingent can scarcely have been larger than the main body of the royal army.

These, however, were the major battles. Lesser engagements, where only a few noblemen or regional levies were involved, were on a very much smaller scale: 1st St Albans in 1455, for example, has been described as little more than a scuffle in a street. Although the opposing forces included three dukes, four earls, a viscount and six barons, it is unlikely that the Yorkists numbered more than 3,000 men and the royalists 2,000. At Blore Heath in 1459, when the rival

Effigy of the Yorkist, Sir William Harcourt (d. 1482).

forces were not yet fully mobilized, and few noblemen were involved; at Mortimer's Cross, in 1461, which was a regional fight between the Welsh and Marcher supporters of York and Lancaster; at Hedgeley Moor and Hexham (1464), where the Nevill troops were attacked by die-hard Lancastrians, who were mostly far from their sources of regional recruitment – in all these battles the forces engaged on either side may well have been numbered in hundreds rather than thousands. In contrast, 2nd St Albans, when Warwick put out all his strength to meet the victorious advance of a large Lancastrian army, probably ranks among the major battles, even if we must reject Gregory's notion of some 200,000 men engaged. So, too, does the Battle of Edgecote in 1469. Although few noblemen were involved on the rebel side, probably every effort had been made to raise the many thousands of Nevill tenants and followers, and those of the allies and dependents of the Nevill family in the north. Facing them, the Earls of Pembroke and Devon probably had sizable contingents from Wales and the west country, perhaps of 2,000 to 3,000 men each, and it is possible (though it can be no more than an educated guess) that as many as 10,000 men were involved.

As with the overall size of the armies, so with casualties. Sheer common sense demands a drastic reduction of the inflated figures given by the chroniclers, otherwise one is left with an unlikely picture of half the adult male population dressing the battlefields with rows of corpses. Gregory tells us, for example, that at the Battle of Mortimer's Cross, the Yorkists slew more than 3,000 of the enemy: this figure is likely to have exceeded the size of the entire Lancastrian army. For only one battle is it difficult to deny that casualties were on an exceptionally large scale. Towton (in 1461) not only involved the largest armies of the entire war, but it lasted an exceptionally long time, and we know from contemporary accounts that the slaughter of the vanquished was unusually heavy. The chroniclers give varying figures of 30,000, 38,000, 36,000 and 35,000 'commoners'. We might be tempted to reject these figures were it not for a statement in an immediately contemporary letter, which says that the dead were 'numbered by the heralds' at 28,000, and this figure is repeated in a statement by Edward IV himself, and in other contemporary letters, obviously drawing from the same source. Even so 28,000 arouses scepticism, and one chronicler's more sober estimate of 9,000 dead – 10 per cent of the combatants – is likely to be nearer the mark. Even this rate of casualties is probably quite exceptional. In most battles the dead were probably to be numbered in hundreds rather than thousands.

A much more rewarding approach to the whole problem of participation in the civil war is to ask a very different question: not 'How many fought?' but 'Who were they, and why did they become involved?'

The nobility were far more heavily concerned than any other social group. This was inevitable. Their political importance, social

THE DUKE OF NORFOLKE
KILLED AT BOSWORTH
FEILD

Jockey of norfolk
For Dickon thy

be not too bold
master is bought
and sold

A sixteenth-century portrait of John Howard, 1st Duke of Norfolk, killed at Bosworth in 1485: Richard III's most loyal supporter among the magnates.

predominance and command of military resources all made it difficult for them to stand on the sidelines. The higher one was up the social scale, the more compelling became the reasons to become involved, and the more difficult it became to remain disengaged. There is not a single magnate family which avoided commitment at some stage. If it so happened, as with the Earl of Westmorland, that the head of the family was too old and infirm to take part in person, then he was usually represented by his heir or some close relative who could take the family's contingents into battle. For the nobility, both the risks and the rewards of participation were correspondingly higher than for members of other social groups.

The nobility became involved from a variety of motives. As we have seen, noble captains were very much prime targets in battle, and casualties were high. To some extent this encouraged the ethics of the vendetta, and it is no surprise to find that the sons of the Lancastrian noblemen killed at 1st St Albans were among the more hawkish members of the court party when fighting was resumed five years later. Success in battle often provided the opportunity to wreak vengeance on captured prisoners for real or pretended wrongs. But for the most part the motives of the nobility in taking sides were less highly charged. Some were influenced by long-standing feuds between families which made them align themselves on whatever side in the national struggle was opposed to their rival's

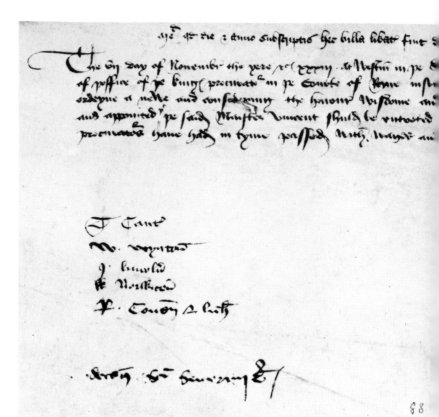

A warrant from the King's Council during the period of the Duke of York's Protectorate, 1454. The councillors present appended their signatures: on the left the bishops, in the centre York and his Nevill friends, 'R. Salisbury' and 'R. Warrewyk'.

interests. The bitter rivalry of Percy and Nevill for predominance in the north of England made them automatic opponents when it came to a choice between York and Lancaster. In the west of England there had been a bitter feud between the Courtenays, Earls of Devon, and the baronial family of Bonville, before the national struggle began. At first Thomas Courtenay, the grasping and ambitious 13th Earl of Devon, supported the Duke of York, while his rival, Lord Bonville, a veteran servant of the House of Lancaster, who had been promoted to his peerage by King Henry VI, clung to the court he had always served. When Devon found that his Yorkist sympathies brought him nothing but grief and imprisonment, he switched sides and fought at 1st St Albans for the king, and the Bonvilles were forced, willy-nilly, into the Yorkist camp. The Bonville heiress (there was no son) married a Nevill, but the old Lord Bonville even then seems to have been inspired by loyalty to the person of Henry VI. He was eventually executed, cruelly and unjustly, after 2nd St Albans on the orders of the Lancastrian Edward, Prince of Wales, who was (so to speak) being given his first 'blooding'.

Most baronial families were influenced by ties of kinship, friendship and marriage. Self-interest, although it played its part, was not necessarily the dominant consideration, and it is striking how, at least in the earlier stages of the war, many noblemen were guided by what they felt to be their allegiance and duty to their anointed king, Henry VI. But the nobility did not always have an entire freedom of choice. Like the gentry, the baronage of any particular region was closely linked by bonds of blood, intermarriage and neighbourliness which could make the ruling class of an entire region swing one way or the other in the civil war. To challenge such regional loyalties could be dangerous as well as uncomfortable, as Lords FitzHugh and Greystoke discovered in 1460–61. Both had connections with the Nevill family, but in a predominantly Lancastrian north, self-preservation compelled them to join Queen Margaret on her march southwards after the Battle of Wakefield. Loyalty to a person or a cause often conflicted with survival or the preservation of the family in the calculations of the average noble-man. Usually, he was realistic enough to accept that there was little to be gained from prolonged adherence to a defeated or discredited cause. After Edward IV's victory at Towton most peers were willing to make peace with the effective king. The world changed: it was prudent to bend with the winds of change. Even so, a significant number of families chose to support the cause of Lancaster to the bitter end, at the cost of life, forfeiture and the ruin of their families. The Wars of the Roses provide plenty of examples of rampant self-interest, of treachery and of cynical changes of side. The contrasting examples of stubborn loyalty to a cause have perhaps not received as much emphasis as they should. The English aristocracy in the later fifteenth century was by no means uniformly selfish or politically cynical.

In the early stages of the civil war, between 1459 and 1461, almost the entire peerage was involved at one stage or another. For the majority, loyalty to the anointed king, Henry VI, seems to have been the main motive, and it was prepared to back its sentiments in arms. Only families which had close and immediate ties of blood and interest with the House of York, like the Nevills and the Bourchiers, supported Duke Richard, although the numbers of Yorkists increased as time wore on. In these years, if we include newly created peers, there were 68 adult noblemen. Of these no less than 53 or 54 took part in the fighting, some on more than one occasion; the majority – about 31 – were Lancastrians. Willingly or unwillingly, therefore, just under four-fifths of the entire peerage was actively involved. Moreover, the absence of the rest can usually be explained by old age, infirmity, idiocy or absence abroad. Almost none of those capable of being involved escaped the fighting, with the notable exception of that classic trimmer, Thomas, Lord Stanley, created Earl of Derby in 1485, who played the shifty role he was to play again in 1470–71 and in 1485. His family motto – *Sans Changer* – could scarcely have been more inappropriate, for the Stanleys owed no loyalty save to themselves.

Many noblemen took part in the fighting in the north in the years 1461–64. Nor had the pattern of aristocratic participation changed much when we come to the next dynastic clash – the round of fighting from Edgecote in 1469 to Tewkesbury in 1471. At least 70 per cent of the nobility were engaged. The reasons for the abstentions are the same as those of 1459–61, and often involved the same old and infirm men.

By 1485 the situation had changed considerably. Dynastic upheavals, deaths in battles, executions for treason and rebellion – all these eroded the traditional sense among the baronage that politics was their natural and normal concern. On the contrary, it was seen to involve increasingly high risks. The Duke of Clarence had been judicially murdered in 1478. Richard III's seizure of power brought with it the execution of Earl Rivers, William, Lord Hastings, and later of the Duke of Buckingham. When the mightiest in the land were so vulnerable, lesser men found it prudent to stand aside if possible. The feeling was exaggerated by Edward IV's policy after 1471 of confining royal patronage to his own family and a small court circle, for fewer noblemen were moved to take part out of gratitude or in the hope of reward. Richard III in his turn was the

The badge of William, Lord Hastings: one of the casualties of Richard III's seizure of the throne.

victim of the violent way in which he usurped the throne. Consequently, rather less than half the peerage (now much reduced in numbers) gave him active support in 1485. Equally, none chose to risk life and fortune by backing the cause of Henry Tudor, except for the already committed Lancastrian exiles like Jasper Tudor, Earl of Pembroke, and Oxford, and the equivocal Stanley. Fewer still of the nobility seem to have taken up arms in the potentially decisive challenge to the crown in 1487. What had been largely lost was the traditional sense of loyalty to an anointed king.

If the nobility were heavily involved, the gentry could scarcely be less so. Nearly all had links with either the king or a nobleman. Many held valuable and lucrative offices in the royal household, in the administration of the Duchy of Lancaster, or in the service of the queen or the Prince of Wales. Many also held office in the estate-organization of a great nobleman or were directly in the receipt of fees and annuities from him. In some parts of the realm, where a single noble interest predominated, it was dangerous not to support one's lord when called upon to do so. There was the risk at least of losing valuable sources of income, and perhaps of even heavier penalties.

Other knights and gentry belonged to families which had long-standing and traditional ties with particular aristocratic families, particularly in areas where these had been dominant for generations. Although, like the nobility, the gentry were often opportunist and self-seeking, there are many instances of dedicated loyalty to the service of a single noble family. The ancestors of William, Lord Hastings, universally admired for his unswerving loyalty to his master, Edward IV, had been the trusted servants of the House of York for four generations. The Yorkshire family of Plumpton was the no less devoted servant of the Percy Earls of Northumberland for more than a century, at the cost of death in battle, attainder and forfeiture, in a pattern which closely parallels the fortunes of its lords.

Obviously, when a lord himself flouted traditional allegiances or was too clearly self-interested, he might forfeit the support of his retainers. The Duke of Clarence's changes of side in the period 1469–71 made his followers reluctant to commit themselves to the fortunes of a weathercock lord. In 1471 the Earl of Northumberland found that he could not persuade his Yorkshire retainers to take up arms on behalf of Edward IV, because so many had lost fathers, brothers or sons in the carnage of Edward's victory at Towton ten years before. Their 'fresh remembrance' of the slaughter meant that 'they could not have borne very good will, and done their best service, to the king at this time and in this quarrel' – so the Yorkist *Arrivall* delicately describes the legacy of hatred which persisted a decade later. The influence of the earl, even in traditionally Percy country, was confined to keeping his men at home. Other gentry families pursued bitter private feuds with their neighbours. Their political allegiances were polarized by those of their enemies. As one turned to Lancaster, so the other supported York, and the baronial feuds, like that of Percy and Nevill, had many a counterpart among the Montagues and Capulets of their gentry connections.

Loyalty, kinship, ambition, self-interest, self-preservation – all this mixture of motives influenced the political allegiances of the landed gentry. But closely involved many of them were, and a considerable number paid the penalty of death in battle, execution afterwards or the confiscation of their estates. At Edgecote Field in 1469 the cream of the Welsh gentry fell in battle. One reliable source lists 23 casualties by name and mentions a further 168 'of the more worthy persons of Wales' who died there. Unfortunately, such precise figures rarely exist for other battles. Scarcely less important than deaths in the fighting, however, were the executions afterwards of captured prisoners. Edward, Earl of March, beheaded 10 knights and esquires from Wales and the English border counties after his victory at Mortimer's Cross in 1461. Some 28 gentry were put to death in the round of executions following the Battle of Hexham in 1464. After Tewkesbury Edward again executed 10 of his captives, but on this occasion spared many more. Some idea of the numbers of gentry involved on the victorious Yorkist side comes from the fact that at the same time he knighted no less than 42 esquires for their share in the battle. In 1470 the government ordered the seizure of the lands of 42 knights, esquires and gentlemen for their support of Warwick and Clarence. Parliamentary sentences of attainder (for which we are on firmer ground as to numbers) tell a very similar story. In Edward IV's reign a total of 38 knights and 55 esquires were attainted, as compared with 16 peers; in that of Richard III, 17 knights and 53 esquires suffered forfeiture for their share in the rebellion of the Duke of Buckingham in 1483.

These figures should be seen in the context of the size of the English gentry class in the mid-fifteenth century. It has been calculated that in 1436 there were only 183 'richer knights' with incomes from land of £200 or more, and that there were about 750 prosperous members of the gentry with incomes between £40 and £100. It is significant that a substantial number of those killed, executed or attainted came from the first group of richer knights, the most substantial of the non-noble·landowners. As the natural leaders of the county establishment, this upper class among the gentry found it as difficult as did the nobility to avoid committing themselves to the civil strife.

In contrast, the English towns strove hard and usually successfully to avoid all but the most token involvement. Most cities, it is true, contained partisans of both sides, and some of the smaller boroughs, within the area of influence of a powerful nobleman, had little choice but to obey his behests. But as corporations the larger towns at least sought to preserve an essential neutrality. In 1471 London fought off the Bastard of Fauconberg's rebels, partly because the fear of pillage and looting stiffened the resolve of the city fathers, though such examples of armed resistance were very rare. Normally a town was willing to open its gates to a near-by victorious army. Occasionally a city showed a marked sympathy with one side or the other. In Canterbury in 1471 the mayor and many of his fellow-townsmen joined the Bastard of Fauconberg in his march on London, and the city was afterwards heavily fined and temporarily lost its privileges as a consequence. Bristol also was fined for giving aid and succour to Queen Margaret's army on her hectic march to Tewkesbury. Later on, the city of York, out of self-interest and in return for his beneficent patronage, became a staunch supporter of King Richard III.

Such behaviour was not typical. The towns often faced agonizing decisions in their efforts to avoid an imprudent show of loyalty to either side in the conflict. In 1470, for example, the city fathers of Salisbury were confronted by rival demands for support from Warwick and Clarence, who had just landed in Devonshire, and from King Edward. Warwick's agent demanded a contingent of forty armed men from them; the king's envoy ordered them to resist the invaders. An attempt to compromise by offering Warwick's man money instead of troops was refused, and in the end the troops were sent, probably because the rebel army was then so much nearer the town than the king, who was still 200 miles away in the north.

In 1471 Salisbury found itself again on the rack of political dilemma. The city fathers agreed to a demand from the restored

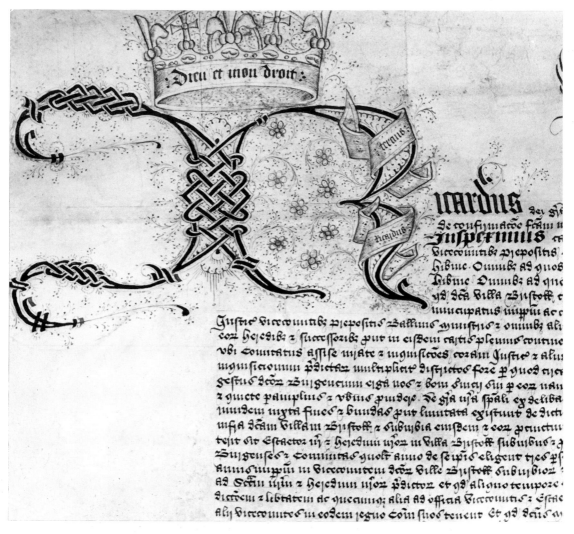

Heading of Richard III's charter to Bristol, 1484. The Yorkist rose with streamers peeps beneath the base of the ornamented initial letter.

government of Henry VI in London to supply it with men, changed their minds when they heard of Edward IV's victory at Barnet, promising him their contingent instead, and changed course once more when they learnt of the landing of Queen Margaret at Weymouth. Their troops, they speciously told the king, were now needed for the defence of the city. Soon they had messengers riding to the Lancastrian Duke of Somerset and the newly Yorkist Duke of Clarence, anxiously explaining why they had sent troops to neither lord. Later there was a nervous wait while another messenger was sent off to Edward IV offering their humble excuses for having failed to proclaim him as king, because, they said hopefully, Queen Margaret was approaching the city with a large army. In the end their entire contribution to the trumpets and alarums of 1471 was to provide the meagre contingent of fourteen men as Edward came close by *en route* to the battlefield of Tewkesbury.

Such lack of militant partisanship explains why the towns in general supplied astonishingly few men to the armies of the civil war. Civic miserliness may have played its part here, since the towns had to finance their own contingents. They obviously resented repeated demands to supply troops for either civil war or the defence of the realm, unless their own interests were directly threatened, and their response was often both grudging and dilatory. King's Lynn sent 25 men to serve Edward IV in 1461, 1462 and 1463, but produced only six in 1469, when he called for help against Robin of Redesdale's rebels; and Richard III got no more than eight in 1483. Norwich, which was then one of the largest towns in England, managed after long delay to produce 120 men for Henry VI in 1461, though the force was taken over by the Yorkists because of the Duke of Norfolk's influence, and fought for Edward IV at Towton. The small size of Norwich's contribution is in striking contrast to the 600 men which it was prepared to supply in 1457, when a French attack on the East Anglian coast was expected, and contrasts also with the host of 1,000 men which John Howard, Duke of Norfolk, expected to raise from his East Anglian estates. Even more revealing is the response of York to King Richard III's appeals for aid in 1485. For all its special ties with him, it produced no more than 80 men at this supreme crisis in its patron's fortunes: and York, like Norwich, was one of the largest cities in the realm. The city records tell us that when news came of Richard's death at Bosworth a 'great heaviness' fell upon the town, but in truth it had scarcely strained its resources to help him.

If the towns contributed far fewer fighting men than might have been expected of them, not surprisingly the great majority of Englishmen who fought in the Wars of the Roses came from the countryside, where 90 per cent of the population lived. The common people of the fifteenth century were noted for being volatile, excitable and turbulent. Accustomed both to bearing arms and to a high level of violence in their daily life, they were prone to join in riots, mob gatherings and insurrections. They could easily be incited to armed action by magnates or gentry whom they admired, by popular preachers, or by real or imagined grievances. They were not without their political consciousness, as Cade's Rebellion and other more local popular movements revealed. Sometimes they had ideas beyond their station. In 1462 there was a number of popular risings in the west country, where the rioters claimed that it was to them that the new king, Edward IV, owed his crown. They also had much less to lose by taking to arms than their social superiors. But for the most part their participation in the campaigns and battles of the civil war sprang less from their own political convictions than from the pressures which the nobility and gentry could exert upon them. They were generally conscripts – perhaps not unwilling conscripts – rather than volunteers. The account-books of John Howard, Duke of Norfolk, reveal that each of the small towns and the villages which lay upon his estates was expected to supply specified contingents to the force of 1,000 men from East Anglia which he expected to command. They also had to pay them, although the lord might supply equipment and even horses, and was often prepared to advance their wages. Such men fought not from choice, but, as the social order of the day demanded, at their lord's demand.

If one compares the English civil wars of the fifteenth with those of the seventeenth century, the great contrast lies in the sporadic nature of the fighting in the earlier conflict. In the reign of Charles I, the fighting was far heavier and more continuous, and it produced essentially professional armies, like Cromwell's famous New Model, which were constantly kept in being. In the fifteenth century, the forces were mostly unprofessional and unpaid, and problems of supply meant that they could not be kept together for more than a few weeks at the very most. The longest campaign of the entire civil war was that of 1471 which lasted from Edward IV's landing on 14 March to his victory at Tewkesbury on 4 May: a total of seven and a half weeks. It has recently been calculated that in some 32 years actual fighting occupied no more than 13 weeks. Because of the highly intermittent nature of the fighting, the impact of civil war on the daily life and security of the ordinary Englishman was much less significant and far reaching than it was to be in the seventeenth century.

Chapter Five

THE IMPACT OF CIVIL WAR ON ENGLISH POLITICS AND SOCIETY

> The most enthusiastic admirer of medieval life must grant that all that was good and great in it was languishing even to death. . . . The sun of the Plantagenets went down in clouds and thick darkness; the coming of the Tudors gave as yet no promise of light; it was 'as the morning spread upon the mountains', darkest before the dawn.

In these somewhat rhetorical phrases, the great Bishop Stubbs, writing his *Constitutional History of England* in 1878, set forth the widely held belief of the Victorians that the Wars of the Roses were an unmitigated catastrophe for England. No one could nowadays be found to argue seriously in favour of this interpretation, for the tendency of modern historians has been to maintain that the consequences of the civil wars were both slight and temporary. But it is possible to go too far in this new direction. In the political sphere at least, the civil wars had results which were at once substantial and long-lasting.

One thing the Wars of the Roses did not do. That ancient and hoary myth – gospel of a hundred textbooks – that they involved 'the suicide of the feudal baronage' and that 'the Tudor despotism' was built upon the ruins of aristocratic power, can now be laid to rest for ever. It has been shown conclusively that there was a very high rate of natural turnover among the English nobility. In each generation of the fourteenth and fifteenth centuries 27 per cent of noble families became extinct. The main reason for this, however, was not death in battle or at the headsman's hands. It was rather the failure of many noblemen to beget male heirs. The two generations between 1450 and 1500 proved no exception to this rule. Thirty-eight families failed in the male line, but only twelve by violence and twenty-six through lack of sons. In spite of heavy casualties, only seven families were extinguished as a direct consequence of civil war, excluding the three royal Houses of Lancaster, York and Beaufort.

There was usually a younger son or brother or a collateral heir to replace a nobleman killed or executed. Three Courtenay Earls of

Devon perished in turn, all of them unmarried, but in 1485 the earldom passed to their kinsman Edward Courtenay of Boconnoc, a descendant of the 10th earl. It was the risky marriage of his son to a daughter of Edward IV which finally brought about the downfall of the family in the reign of Henry VIII. Casualties in the Nevill family were similarly high, among them the Earl of Salisbury and his sons Warwick and Montagu. Yet even if Warwick had not been killed at Barnet, the chances of there being a male heir to his wealthy earldom were small. He had been married for twenty years, his wife was forty-six, and their sole issue had been two daughters. Montagu's branch of the family failed not because of his death in battle but because his son, George, died without male heirs in 1483.

Even where families were exterminated, died out from natural causes or went into long-term exile, new ones rose to take their place. Henry VI had been lavish in creating new peers, and the political insecurity of the Yorkist kings forced them to continue the same policy. Edward IV ennobled or promoted no less than thirty-two peers, including four dukes and ten earls. Nor did the disappearance of a powerful family necessarily leave any gap in the ranks of the aristocracy. Thus Richard III's urgent need for support led him to allow the great Mowbray dukedom of Norfolk to pass to his ally, John Howard, and Howard's son became Earl of Surrey. The Howards survived the discomforts of 1485 to become a major force in the power-politics of the Tudor court.

Nevertheless, the political influence of the aristocracy was severely reduced as a direct consequence of the Wars of the Roses. In part, this was due to the changing attitudes of the peers themselves (see above, pp. 144–45). By 1485 noblesse oblige no longer included an unquestioning and committed loyalty to the reigning king. Many peers had become disenchanted with politics, and would have agreed with the advice given by Lord Mountjoy to his son, that it was unwise 'to be great about princes, for it is dangerous'. In part, it was due to the policies of the first two Tudor kings. Edward IV had not overtly set out to reduce aristocratic power, rather the reverse, but a significantly larger proportion of the higher nobility were either 'new men' of his own creation, like William Herbert, Earl of Pembroke, or, like Clarence, Gloucester and Rivers, members of the royal family, who owed their power and eminence to the king himself, rather than to inherited wealth and power. Richard III had neither the time nor the opportunity to strike at the foundations of aristocratic power. Henry VII, however, deliberately set about eroding the capacity of the nobility to disrupt the peace of the realm. He created very few new peers, and conspicuously failed to fill vacancies in their ranks which came about by natural wastage. Of the twenty families which made up the higher nobility (dukes, earls and marquises) in 1485, only half still held their titles in 1509. Even more important, Henry set about disciplining and intimidating the nobility by a systematic use of suspended sentences of attainder, and by forcing them to enter

Opposite: officials of Edward IV's royal household, from the *Black Book* of *c.* 1472. The captions suggest the virtues they should possess, Circumspection, Discretion and Intelligence, for example.

Domus Prouidentiæ.

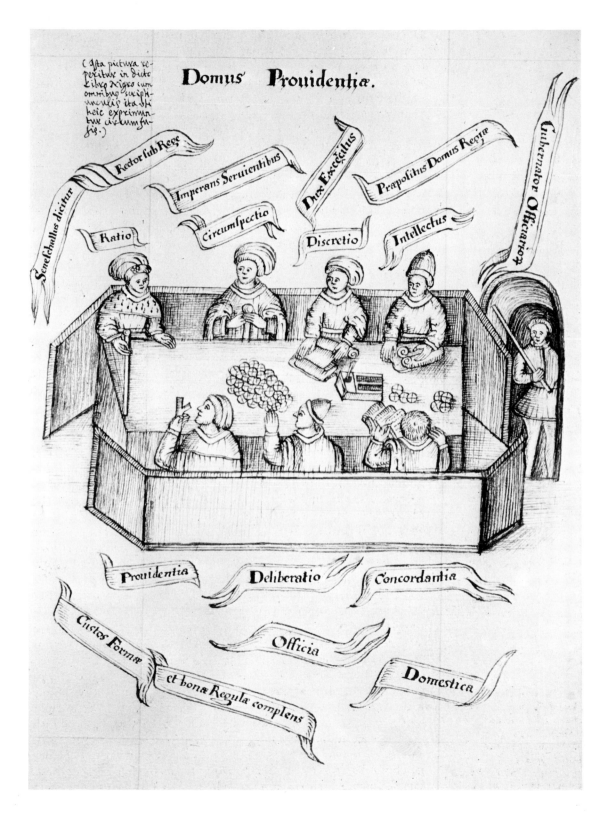

(Ista pictura reperitur in dicto Libro Nigro cum omnibus scripturiculis ita sic heic exprimitur circumfig.)

Seneschallus dicitur

Rector sub Rege

Imperans Seruientibus

Dux Excellus

Praepositus Domus Regiæ

Gubernator Officiariorum

Ratio

Circumspectio

Discretio

Intellectus

Prouidentia   Deliberatio   Concordantia

Custos Formæ

et bonæ Regulæ complens   Officia   Domestica

Opposite: emblems of Henry VII and Elizabeth of York on quarries at Westminster Abbey, sixteenth century. The portcullis of the Beaufort family is prominent in the centre.

Henry VII by P. Torrigiano, *c.* 1512–18, from his tomb at Westminster Abbey.

into a terrifying system of bonds and recognizances, which threatened them with crushing financial penalties if they misbehaved or offended the king. By 1509 few noble families had escaped this iron spider's web of royal control, and the nobility were in even more chastened mood than they had been in 1485.

Much of the success of this suspicious, energetic and determined king can be explained in terms of his own ability; and his high-handed treatment of the nobility was maintained by his even more domineering and ruthless son, Henry VIII. But both Tudor kings were aided by the newly craven mood in which the nobility confronted their rule. They were helped even more by the havoc which the Wars of the Roses had wrought among the *upper* ranks of the aristocracy. In the late Lancastrian and Yorkist period there were at various times about a dozen magnates of high birth who commanded the wealth, estates and local influence which enabled them to challenge the king in arms. Among them the Dukes of York, Buckingham, Somerset, Norfolk, Clarence and Gloucester, and the Earls of Warwick and Northumberland. By 1509 only two of these powerful families – Buckingham and Northumberland – survived with their power intact; and the estates, and with them the local influence, of almost all the others had come into the firm possession of the king. For all their wealth and influence, the leading members of the Tudor nobility were much more creatures of the court, and much less the semi-independent regional princes that their fifteenth-century pre-

Silver groat of Henry VII,
c. 1500.

decessors had been. The Tudor nobility had largely lost both the
power and the inclination to take up arms against the king. Successive noblemen were condemned for treason and executed by Henry
VII and Henry VIII without making a fight of it, and the only
Tudor rebellion which can bear comparison with the aristocratic
risings which so disturbed the fifteenth century was that of the
Northern Earls in 1569. This was the direct product of Elizabeth I's
policy, which left them little choice but to defend themselves in
arms. The disappearance of the higher nobility as rivals to the royal
authority, and of their capacity to disrupt normal political life by
force, marks a momentous change in the character of English politics.
In many ways it can be regarded as a consequence of the civil war
of the fifteenth century.

The effects of the civil war on the English landowning classes –
the gentry as well as the nobility – might have been far more serious
if kings had been less generous to their opponents and more rigorous

in upholding sentences of forfeiture for treason. Such sentences of attainder were the usual penalty for backing the wrong side, and, if upheld, spelt not only the punishment of the individual offender, but the permanent ruin of his entire family and the confiscation of all his possessions. In practice, however, the weakness of usurping kings, and their urgent need to reconcile opponents and win support, made it possible to get attainders reversed, although Henry VII was far tougher in this respect than the Yorkists had been. Sometimes also it was difficult to recover one's property when it had been granted to powerful men. But few families were ruined by attainders. Between 1459 and 1509 397 persons (excluding royalty) were attainted. Of these 256 (64 per cent) had their sentences reversed. The higher a man's social status, the easier it was to get a sentence set aside. Of the attainted peers, over 84 per cent secured reversals, although some had to wait a long time. So, too, did 79 per cent of the knights and 76 per cent of the esquires, followed at a considerable distance by lesser ranks.

Even if its effects were only temporary, however, the system of attainders involved the transfer of huge quantities of land from old owners to new. These changes brought with them crucial crises of loyalty for the retainers, dependents and tenants of a dispossessed family. Their responses varied according to circumstances. In some parts of the country loyalty to a particular family was ingrained and traditional. Any allegiance to a new lord was likely to be brittle and short-lived, especially if the heir of a disinherited family was still alive, and there was a reasonable chance of his being restored. If, on the other hand, he was an obdurate rebel, in exile for thirty years or more (like the Roos and Beaumont families in the Midlands), then old loyalties might be worn down by a sense of hopelessness and sheer passage of time. They could rarely be reversed in a few years. Much depended on the power and personality of the new incumbent. Lord Hastings' enormous influence at court made it possible for him to build up a reliable following on the basis of forfeited lands in the Midlands, among them the Roos and Beaumont estates: his 'good lordship' was well worth having. Duke Richard of Gloucester was able to win the loyalty of former followers of the Nevills in the north of England, partly because his wife was a Nevill heiress, and partly because his service offered remarkable opportunities for advancement and profit. But John, Marquis Montagu, was less successful in diverting Percy sympathies in the north-east, and a restoration of the Percy heir ultimately became politically essential. More short-lived attempts to secure a general transfer of loyalty, like Richard III's northern 'colonization' of the southern and western counties, had no success at all. Probabl it was these rapid changes in local lordship rather than the political changes at the centre which made many a gentleman sleep uneasy in his bed.

By choice or necessity, kings, noblemen and gentry were the people most immediately involved in both the military and political aspects of the civil war, and the effects upon them were correspondingly greater. Other influential groups within the political community – the high clergy, the lawyers and the merchants – almost entirely escaped involvement. In the factious later years of Henry VI appointments to bishoprics, normally the preserve of the king in person, became something of a prize for contending parties. The result was the appointment of prelates who were politically involved, some of them members of the high aristocracy. So Duke Richard of York used his first period of power in 1454–55 to promote his kinsman Thomas Bourchier to the see of Canterbury, which he was to hold under no less than five kings. During York's second protectorate Nevill influence secured the appointment of Warwick's under-age brother, George, to the see of Exeter. Both were prominent partisans of the Yorkist cause in the years which followed. The main body of bishops, however, in spite of the fact that they owed their promotions to Henry VI or his court, made little attempt to oppose the Yorkist seizure of power in 1460–61, and, apart from George Nevill, by then Archbishop of York, they played equally little part in the revolutions of 1469–71. In the second half of his reign Edward IV acquired a tighter control over the bench of bishops. His new appointments were mostly career prelates, predominantly trained as canon or civil lawyers, who were administrators, diplomats or civil servants: scarcely any were aristocrats. Most of them were prepared to make themselves useful to whichever king sat on the throne. These episcopal Vicars of Bray did not oppose Richard III's usurpation. Only when Buckingham rebelled in 1483 did the upper clergy play any significant part. John Morton, Bishop of Ely, was a kind of *éminence grise* in stirring up the rebellion; Lionel Woodville of Salisbury had obvious links with a rising in which his mother and brother were closely involved; and Peter Courtenay of Exeter was similarly linked by blood with some of the west-country rebels. In 1485 the bishops accepted Henry VII's accession with equanimity. But the reluctance of the upper clergy to become involved did not prevent many of the clerical proletariat from taking sides in the struggle. The names of parish priests and chaplains are often prominent in lists of indicted rebels, and the pulpit may have been a more potent weapon than we know in rousing a volatile populace to take up arms.

As befitted their profession, the lawyers were more cautious still. When Duke Richard claimed the throne in 1460, first the king's judges and then the serjeants-at-law were asked for their opinions. Without hesitation, they answered that such high matters as concerned the king's estate were 'above the law and beyond their learning', and it was left to the Lords, to their dismay, to refute his pretensions if they could. The reward of prudence was security of tenure. It was said that Chief Justice Markham was dismissed from the King's Bench because he refused to bring in a charge of treason against a former Mayor of London, Sir Thomas Cook, whose head

Opposite: Richard III and his queen, Anne Nevill, daughter of Warwick the Kingmaker (see p. 33). Her death in 1484 led to rumours that Richard intended to marry his niece, Elizabeth of York, later queen of Henry VII.

Ricardus tercius Dei gra Rex
Anglie et Francie et Dns Hibrnie

Dna Anna filia Dni Comitis Warwici
Dei gra Regina Anglie et Francie et Dna Hibrnie

the Woodville family wanted brought to them upon a charger. Otherwise judges and senior lawyers kept their posts without difficulty. For example, Sir William Hussey, whom Edward IV promoted to be Chief Justice of the King's Bench in 1481, was reappointed under Edward V, Richard III and Henry VII, and held office, plumply prosperous, until his death or retirement in 1495.

The merchant oligarchies who controlled the larger towns were, as we have seen, largely successful in keeping their cities clear of military involvement in the conflict. This achieved, their interest lay in the country's commercial activities which sustained their prosperity. These were only marginally affected by the fighting. In 1459–61, and again in 1469–71, there was some interference in the export of English wool to its main market at Calais, which was temporarily in the hands of the government's opponents. Otherwise trade went on as before. A far greater worry was the economic depression, particularly in foreign trade, which began about 1450 and lasted until 1475. For this the Lancastrian government was largely to blame. Bad foreign relations, unwise commercial policies, the lack of control of piracy by Englishmen on the high seas – all contributed to a decline in every branch of foreign trade. One reason why the Londoners in particular tended to favour the Yorkist cause was the hope that a change of government might bring about better commercial prospects. King Edward IV, who himself engaged largely in foreign trade, eventually did much to restore prosperity by keeping the peace abroad and through a series of commercial treaties with England's trading neighbours. The great improvement in trade which marked his later years continued unchecked by the political upheavals of the years 1483–87. For the merchant class in general, the commercial policies of successive governments were of far greater importance than the civil war.

At the highest political level, both crown and Parliament were affected by the civil war. The authority of Parliament, as the highest court of the realm, was thought essential to legitimize major political changes and such matters as the confirmation of royal titles and Acts of Attainder. This encouraged both sides in the conflict to attempt to 'pack' Parliament in their own interest, in order to secure a complacent House of Commons. Interference in elections was made easier by the fact that a great many borough seats, which formed some two-thirds of the House of Commons, were already attached to 'rotten' or 'pocket' boroughs – most of them, like Old Sarum in Wiltshire, were to survive until swept away by the Reform Act of 1832. Such places could readily be persuaded to accept as their MPs outsiders, royal servants or the retainers and hangers-on of the nobility. If the king and his great lords worked in harmony, they could often secure something like a 'working majority' in the House of Commons. Thus the Parliament of 1478, summoned to condemn the Duke of Clarence for treason, contained 57 members (about 20 per cent of the entire house) who were royal servants: 43 of these

Opposite: the introduction to the declaration of Henry VII's title in the Parliament of 1485; from the Statute Roll of that year.

were officials of the royal household. Many other seats were held by followers of the Woodville family (Clarence's declared enemies), or of the Duke of Gloucester and other noblemen who supported the king. Not surprisingly, this packed House had no qualms about sanctioning the very one-sided proceedings against Clarence; and when the king delayed in carrying out the death-sentence, it was a deputation from the Commons which called upon him to do so. In general, the Parliaments of this period were entirely complacent about endorsing each change of regime, each indictment of the vanquished. With great equanimity, they reversed the acts of previous Parliaments for the benefit of whichever new party was in power.

The Commons lost initiative as well as independence as a direct consequence of the civil war. Governments anxious to put through measures vital to their interests began to take an increasing interest in the management of the Commons' business. Major bills were often drafted and presented by the king and his Council, while genuine 'Commons' bills' were quite often rejected if they happened not to suit the king's interest. Not surprisingly, it was during this period that the Speaker of the Commons, who was nearly always a member of the King's Council, and was paid for his services as Speaker from 1461, began to emerge as something resembling a modern Leader of the House of Commons, responsible for the organization and management of government business.

Ultimately, one of the main political consequences of the civil war was an increase in the personal and prerogative power of the king. Contemporaries were only too well aware of the evils which had flowed from the personal weakness of Henry VI. They saw clearly that the curbing of private feud and faction, the repression of riot and gangsterism, and the correction of injustice could only come from a more vigorous and impartial exercise of the royal authority. Most Englishmen were willing to support a king who could offer these benefits, and this feeling strengthened as the civil strife continued.

In the first decade of his reign Edward IV failed to win the confidence of his subjects, but after 1471 he ruled with greater firmness and authority. It remained difficult to obtain redress at law against a great man who enjoyed the king's confidence, for Edward's concern for justice certainly did not extend to weakening the authority of his own supporters, but at least he was able to reduce the level of violence and oppression. He managed to combine this with the avoidance of expensive foreign wars, a low level of taxation and the encouragement of English commerce. The fact that he could also be arbitrary and that he was in no way checked or controlled by Parliament did nothing to detract from his subjects' admiration, since he brought them a measure of civil order and prosperity. An increase in the power of the crown was considered a small price to pay for domestic peace. Henry VII was far less popular than Edward

IV had been, but he followed many of the same policies with even greater firmness, and his increasingly harsh and suspicious rule was accepted for the same reasons. The deep respect of Tudor Englishmen for authority thus had a firm historical basis in the fear of political dissension engendered by the Wars of the Roses.

For the ordinary, politically inconspicuous Englishman the effects of civil war were much less direct than for his social superiors. English life and civilization in general were remarkably little affected by thirty years of sporadic conflict. There was very little material devastation, little pillaging or plundering, certainly nothing to compare with the systematic destruction of people, buildings, stock and crops which the English armies had been wont to inflict on many parts of France during the Hundred Years War, the effects of which were still being felt many years later. There was no *general* collapse of law and order, save perhaps for brief periods in 1459–61 and 1469–71. No major English town was looted or pillaged, or even systematically besieged.

The armies might fight, but the farmer continued to sow; from a fifteenth-century glass roundel.

163

Powerful men could not always be persuaded to divert their energies into such (relatively) peaceful pursuits as the tournament. Here knights make their way through London to one of these military sporting occasions, c. 1460–80.

For most Englishmen the chief social evil of the day was the ability of powerful men to defy the law, to bend or pervert the course of justice and to use violence in pursuit of their own interests or those of their followers. The records of the time abound with murders, beatings-up, the destruction of manor-houses, the carrying-away of stock and such-like misdeeds, performed by large gangs of armed men. Most of these were acting on the orders, or were under the protection of, a powerful patron who could secure their immunity from reprisal or intimidate the victims into keeping silent. Under such protection, some men became almost professional criminals and gangsters who were able to evade the always inefficient clutches of the law for long periods at a time. One such was Sir Thomas Malory, the distinguished author of the *Morte D'Arthur*. Although he sat in Parliament on no less than three occasions, Malory was also a flagrant law-breaker. In late 1449 or early 1450, with a gang of twenty-six men, he tried to ambush and murder the Duke of Buckingham; in May 1450 he committed rape and extortion, and again in August. Next year he stole several hundred head of livestock, terrorized the monks of Monks Kirby, stole deer from the Duke of Buckingham's park at Caludon, broke into Combe Abbey to steal money and ornaments, and came back the next day with a hundred men to insult the monks and steal more money. His crimes eventually landed him in gaol – to which we owe the *Morte D'Arthur* – although he was twice bailed out and twice escaped. Other and better-connected offenders pursued criminal careers with greater impunity. The Cornishman Sir Henry Bodrugan was denounced in Parliament in 1459 as a notorious malefactor. Yet he was still at large some thirty years later, having maintained a minor reign of terror in parts of Cornwall, and in spite of being repeatedly charged with murder, piracy, extortion, fraud and intimidation. Only an unwise adherence to the cause of Richard III put an end to the career of this successful gangster. Throughout, his connections with the Yorkist court enabled him to secure repeated pardons for his offences: he even contrived to be knighted by the king at the creation of the Prince of Wales.

The high level of violence which characterized late-medieval society, and the difficulties of obtaining justice, were, however, not products of the civil war. They were rooted in the social structure of fifteenth-century England, above all in the local power of great men who had the ear and the protection of the central power. They were reinforced by the complexities of the common law (which contained all sorts of built-in means to pervert or delay the course of justice), by the weakness of the machinery of law-enforcement and by the venality and corruptibility of local officials. Such abuses were nothing new in 1455, for they had been repeatedly denounced by the Commons in Parliament for several decades previously. One of the most notorious examples of a regime of local oppression and intimidation belongs to the 1440s, when the 'heavy lordship' of the Duke of Suffolk and his agents was felt throughout East Anglia.

No doubt the outbreak of civil war tended to make such evils worse, at least during the two phases of heavy fighting at the beginning and the end of Edward IV's first decade. Private feuds could be pursued with greater impunity under the umbrella of national conflict. For example, the Duke of Norfolk chose the troubled summer of 1469 to besiege and capture the Paston family's castle of Caister. In Gloucestershire in 1470 the long rivalry between the Berkeley and Talbot families exploded into a pitched battle between their partisans, and in Lancashire the Stanleys and the Harringtons resorted to violence in a bitter inheritance dispute. In Oxfordshire the Staffords of Grafton took the opportunity to revenge the murder of Sir Humphrey Stafford by Sir Richard Harcourt in 1448: Harcourt was murdered in his turn by Sir Humphrey's bastard son. More important, as the aristocratic factions became polarized round national leaders, governments became more dependent on their own partisans, and proved increasingly reluctant to punish them for their misdeeds. Henry VI's ministers, for example, would not act against the Earl of Devon in the 1450s despite the open contempt for the law shown by him – among the earl's exploits were the brutal murder of his father-in-law, a forcible entry into Exeter Cathedral, and a siege of Powderham Castle near Exeter, which belonged to one of his kinsmen. Edward IV was sharply prepared to take action against riots and assemblies which savoured of Lancastrian partisanship or of treason, but noticeably non-punitive against the 'heavy lordship' of his own supporters. The worst examples of unchecked lawlessness belong, however, to the period 1450–70, when government was at its weakest and faction at its height. There was a general improvement after 1471, which continued under Henry VII. The abuse of private power was in any case something which Englishmen had long since learned to live with: the civil war merely served to make it more blatant.

'A low level of public security', observed K. B. McFarlane, 'was not incompatible with a vigorous national life', and it is indeed true that English civilization was remarkably little affected by the civil wars. Large areas of the country were untouched by essentially sporadic campaigning spread over thirty years, and, if there was a higher level of lawlessness and disorder, it does not seem to have affected men's attitudes towards the arts of peace. This fact is strikingly demonstrated by the history of English domestic building in the second half of the fifteenth century. In a world supposedly torn by civil strife, men showed little interest in the defence of their homes. The nobility continued to build castles, and the wealthier gentry fortified manor-houses, but these were very different from the grim, comfortless and often impregnable fortresses of an earlier age. At first sight the most elaborate of the mid- and late-fifteenth-century castles present an imposing appearance, but in practice their defensive capacity was limited, for their builders were often more concerned with magnificence and comfort. The great brick tower of Ralph, Lord Cromwell, at Tattershall in Lincolnshire looks initially formidable, but the walls conceal elegant apartments, the battlements hide a roof-garden, and the task of the defender was seriously hampered by an arcaded gallery running right round the inside of the walls. Here and elsewhere the defensive qualities of the building were severely reduced by the growing fashion for large windows, which made them highly vulnerable to cannon-fire. Even the wide wet moats, like that at Hurstmonceux in Sussex, seem to have been valued for setting off the attractions of the building, reflected in their quiet waters. Another new fashion, for building imposing gatehouses, was inspired less by a concern for defence than by a desire for display and to provide the family and its guests with private quarters, separate from the accommodation of servants and retainers. One of the latest of these structures, Oxburgh Hall in Norfolk, completed in 1480, has a towering and impressive seven-storey gatehouse. It served to impress the beholder with the wealth and dignity of its builders, the gentry family of Bedingfield, but the air of military strength it suggests is largely an illusion.

Opposite: Tattershall Castle, Lincolnshire, built by Lord Cromwell: an early example of castle-building in brick. The wide windows, even at ground level, suggest a concern for light and comfort rather than defence.

Left: the entrance tower of Ightham Mote, Kent (1480), a typical small gatehouse of the period. *Below:* Hurstmonceux Castle, Sussex, dating from the second quarter of the fifteenth century. *Opposite:* the gatehouse of Raglan Castle, Monmouthshire, completed in the 1460s. In all three buildings the windows reduced the capacity for defence, especially against gunfire.

Far away in the wilder conditions of the Welsh Marches, the elegant castle, copied from French models, which William, Lord Herbert, completed at Raglan in the 1460s, is a more serious affair, with a strong central keep and a cunningly designed gatehouse, but even here a concern for comfort shows in the wide windows, the fine fireplaces and the elaborate decoration of the main apartments. Not far away from Raglan, at Tretower Court, the Herberts' humbler kinsmen, the Vaughan family, were prepared to risk building a house with only the most token fortifications. Its tiny battlemented gatehouse might have enabled the occupants to hold off an attack by casual marauders for a short time, but the rest of the house with its spacious timbered hall, its private bedchambers and guest-rooms with their windows, and its solar (or sun-room) entirely sacrificed defence to improved standards of domestic comfort. The entire building forms a sharp contrast with the grim and comfortless shell-keep of Tretower Castle a hundred yards away: this former Vaughan residence no longer satisfied the more luxurious standards of fifteenth-century England.

Only in the north did the nobility continue to occupy the still powerful fortresses left them by earlier generations, but even these were internally remodelled and modernized to provide greater standards of ease, convenience and privacy. At Nottingham Castle, for example, King Edward IV, who was more concerned than most with his creature comforts, built himself a new polygonal tower with 'marvellous fair' windows and chambers, later described 'as the

Tretower Court, in the Welsh Marches, with its rather half-hearted fortifications.

most beautifullest and gallant building for lodging'. No word is said about its capacity to resist attack. Everywhere south of the Trent, however, the needs of defence tended to become a secondary consideration. Here and there it was totally ignored. At Ockwells in Berkshire John Norris was able to build a fine manor-house, completed about 1465, whose timbered hall, with its series of great gabled and mullioned rectangular windows, made no pretensions to defensibility. It is the direct ancestor of the great country-houses of Tudor England. Similar houses, like that of the Greville family in Chipping Camden, were being built in unwalled towns, or, like that of William Canynges in the Bristol suburbs, in towns where the fortifications had long been allowed to decay, and where the authorities remained totally unwilling to spend money on their repair.

The sense of physical security which possessed the English propertied classes during this phase of civil war is highlighted even further by their indifference to changes in the art of war, particularly the advance of artillery. In some parts of the Continent, especially Italy, many fortresses were being totally remodelled to make them at once less vulnerable to gunfire and capable of defending themselves with cannon. King Edward IV did indeed experiment with such practices at the Tower of London and in the English fortresses in the Calais region. But few private builders followed his example, with the partial exception of his devoted friend and disciple,

The upstairs rooms, drawing-rooms and chambers, originally divided, at Tretower Court (behind the wooden gallery on p. 170); designed for comfort rather than military needs.

Opposite: Kirby Muxloe, started by Lord Hastings but left incomplete after his execution: notable for its use of brick, as well as for its gunports near ground level.

Huish Episcopi, Somerset; one of the many fine church-towers built in the West Country and elsewhere during the second half of the fifteenth century.

William, Lord Hastings, whose castle at Kirby Muxloe (1483–84) was almost the only one of the period to include gunports for defensive cannon in its lower ranges, although the rest of the structure was indefensible by contemporary Italian standards.

The arts of peace in general were scarcely touched by civil war. Political violence did not prevent Englishmen from rebuilding and embellishing their parish churches on a large scale, nor from founding a profusion of colleges, chantries and schools. Architecturally, the period of civil war saw the flowering of the Perpendicular or Late Gothic style which reached its culmination in such buildings as Edward IV's Chapel of St George at Windsor, King's College, Cambridge, and the supremely elegant towers of so many Somerset churches. The calm and dignified lines of these structures, full of a new spaciousness and light, were offset by a wealth of elaborate decoration in stone and timber sculpture, and in stained and painted glass. Indeed, in woodcarving and glassmaking English craftsmen reached a perfection rarely equalled and never surpassed in this

Caxton's woodcut of a blacksmith; from his *Game and Play of the Chess*, 1483.

country. The overall effect is one of dignified richness and elegant luxury. Like the great Georgian country-houses and terraces of eighteenth-century England, these fifteenth-century buildings reflect a society assured of its values and essentially self-confident.

Historians of architecture tell us that there was a marked decline in the pace of building during the Wars of the Roses, beginning in the 1450s, with recovery setting in only with the return of more peaceful conditions in the 1470s. To some extent this claim can be justified, though there are many notable exceptions, but the cause was rather the economic depression of the period which affected the resources of the propertied classes. The expansion of building activity coincides almost exactly with the return of economic prosperity in the second decade of Edward IV's reign. Only here and there did political conflict impinge on all this activity. At King's College, Cambridge, for example, which was founded by Henry VI in 1441, building works were interrupted first by the growing impoverishment of the crown in the king's later years and then by

the hostility which Edward IV showed towards a Lancastrian foundation. Only towards the end of his reign was building resumed, to be completed under the Tudor kings. But such examples are rare.

Nor does the literature of the period reflect any great concern with civil war. This was an age of steadily advancing vernacular culture, expressing itself in the ballads, lyrics, carols and play-cycles popular with the ordinary people, in the histories, chronicles and didactic treatises favoured by the merchants, and in the chivalric romances, now increasingly being translated into English from their original French and Burgundian versions, enjoyed by the court and the nobility. The diffusion of literacy was enhanced by the foundation of William Caxton's printing-press in London in the later years of Edward IV. It is true that some of this literature, particularly the poetry, is affected by a strain of melancholy, of pessimism and a morbid concern with death. In part these sentiments were inherited from an earlier age, in part they reflect a sense of the transience of earthly life natural in a society vulnerable to plague and famine and

The Squire, a woodcut from Caxton's edition of Chaucer's *Canterbury Tales*. Printing was one of the many arts of peace that flourished during the Wars of the Roses.

a high level of day-to-day violence. But the horrors of civil war are not one of literature's themes, if we exclude the expressly political songs and ballads which often had a propaganda purpose. It was left to the writers of the Tudor period, harassed by their own fears of insecurity, to make a literary mountain out of the ravages of 'intestinal division'. Those who lived through the civil war evidently felt no such need. England in the later fifteenth century was, in fact, the home of a rich, varied and vigorous civilization. To study it is to remain largely unaware that it was the product of an age of political violence, which did nothing to hinder its steady development.

A scene from Caxton's book on chess, *c.* 1482; one of the early products of his printing press.

Opposite: Late Perpendicular architecture reached heights of elaborate perfection during the Wars. Here, the marvellous fan-vault of Sherborne Abbey; last quarter of the fifteenth century.

TABLE I: THE HOUSES OF LANCASTER, TUDOR AND BEAUFORT

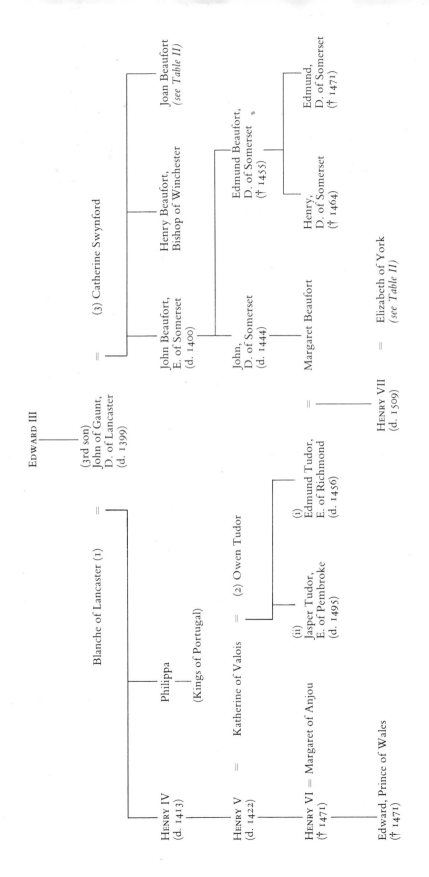

† Death other than by natural causes

TABLE II: THE HOUSES OF YORK AND NEVILL

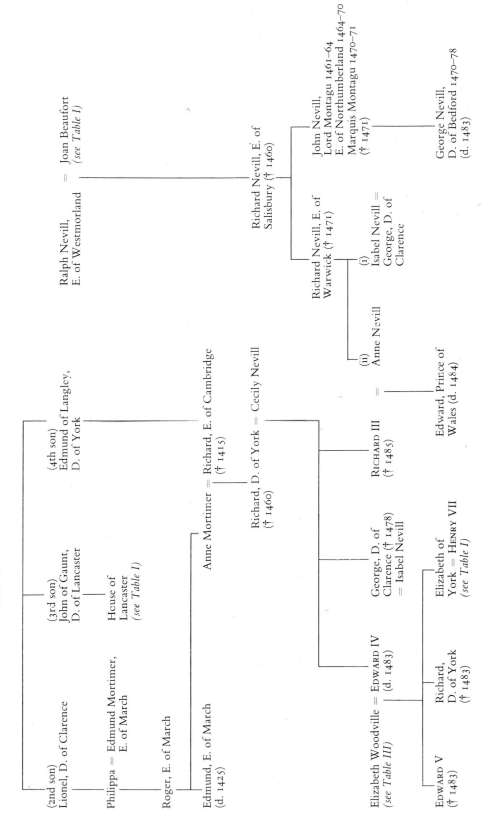

Edward III

(2nd son)
Lionel, D. of Clarence

Philippa = Edmund Mortimer,
E. of March

Roger, E. of March

Edmund, E. of March
(d. 1425)

(3rd son)
John of Gaunt,
D. of Lancaster

House of
Lancaster
(see Table I)

(4th son)
Edmund of Langley,
D. of York

Anne Mortimer = Richard, E. of Cambridge
(† 1415)

Richard, D. of York = Cecily Nevill
(† 1460)

Elizabeth Woodville = EDWARD IV
(see Table III)   (d. 1483)

George, D. of
Clarence († 1478)
= Isabel Nevill

RICHARD III
(† 1485)

Elizabeth of
York = HENRY VII
(see Table I)

Richard,
D. of York
(† 1483)

EDWARD V
(† 1483)

Edward, Prince of
Wales (d. 1484)

Ralph Nevill, = Joan Beaufort
E. of Westmorland   (see Table I)

Richard Nevill, E. of
Salisbury († 1460)

Richard Nevill, E. of
Warwick († 1471)

(i)
Isabel Nevill =
George, D. of
Clarence

(ii)
Anne Nevill

John Nevill,
Lord Montagu 1461–64
E. of Northumberland 1464–70
Marquis Montagu 1470–71
(† 1471)

George Nevill,
D. of Bedford 1470–78
(d. 1483)

TABLE III: THE WOODVILLE CONNECTIONS OF EDWARD IV

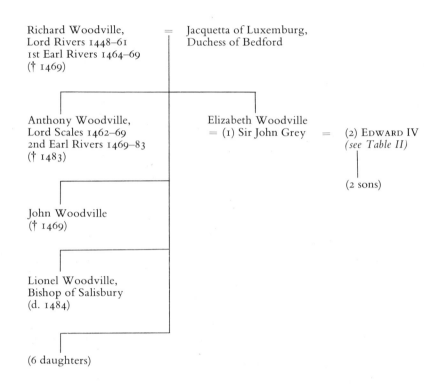

Richard Woodville,
Lord Rivers 1448–61
1st Earl Rivers 1464–69
(† 1469)

= Jacquetta of Luxemburg,
Duchess of Bedford

Anthony Woodville,
Lord Scales 1462–69
2nd Earl Rivers 1469–83
(† 1483)

Elizabeth Woodville
= (1) Sir John Grey

= (2) EDWARD IV
(see Table II)

(2 sons)

John Woodville
(† 1469)

Lionel Woodville,
Bishop of Salisbury
(d. 1484)

(6 daughters)

BIBLIOGRAPHY

An admirable and lively survey of the fifteenth century in general may be found in J. R. Lander, *Conflict and Stability in Fifteenth-Century England* (London: Hutchinson, 1969). A more political but very useful account is by S. B. Chrimes, *Lancastrians, Yorkists and Henry VII* (London: Macmillan, 1964). Fuller, but rather dull and lacking in incisive judgments, is E. F. Jacob, *The Fifteenth Century* (Oxford: Clarendon Press, 1961). Much of value can still be found in two remarkable essays, one by K. B. McFarlane, 'The Lancastrian Kings', and the other by C. H. Williams, 'The Yorkist Kings', both in the *Cambridge Medieval History*, vol. VIII (Cambridge: University Press, 1936).

The Wars of the Roses have rarely been treated as a separate theme. J. R. Lander's *The Wars of the Roses* (London: Secker and Warburg, 1965) provides a narrative by stringing together extracts from contemporary sources, with a useful short introduction. Hubert Cole, *The Wars of the Roses* (London: Hart-Davis, McGibbon, 1973) is an exclusively narrative and rather old-fashioned treatment, which includes no consideration of the wider aspects of the subject. A. L. Rowse's *Bosworth Field and the Wars of the Roses* (London: Macmillan, 1966), despite its title, offers a lengthy narrative of English history from 1377 to 1485 intended to show that Shakespeare's interpretation of the period was correct. By far the best essay of synthesis is the illuminating study by K. B. McFarlane in his 'The Wars of the Roses', *Proceedings of the British Academy*, vol. L (1964), and much other material may be found in his *Nobility of Later Medieval England* (Oxford: Clarendon Press, 1973).

For the origins of the war, R. L. Storey provides an invaluable if controversial study in his *End of the House of Lancaster* (London: Barrie and Rockliff, 1966), which should be supplemented by two useful special studies by R. A. Griffiths, 'Local Rivalries and National Politics: The Percies, the Nevilles, and the Duke of Exeter, 1452–1455', *Speculum*, vol. XLIII (1968), and 'Duke Richard of York's intentions in 1450, and the origins of the Wars of the Roses', *Journal of Medieval History*, vol. I (1975). C. A. J. Armstrong, 'Politics and the Battle of St. Albans, 1455', *Bulletin of the Institute of Historical Research*, vol. XXXIII (1960) is also very valuable for the immediate preliminaries to the fighting. For the civil war in the Yorkist period (1461–71) the most recent account is by Charles Ross, *Edward IV* (London: Eyre Methuen; Berkeley: University of California Press; 1974), and for the final phases (1483–87) see J. Gairdner, *Richard III* (Cambridge: University Press, 1898), P. M. Kendall, *Richard III* (London: George Allen and Unwin, 1955), and S. B. Chrimes, *Henry VII* (London: Eyre Methuen; Berkeley: University of California Press; 1972), which has a scholarly account of the Bosworth campaign.

Like the history of the civil war in general, its military aspects have never been treated as a whole. Some rather misleading comments are to be found in C. W. C. Oman's *The Art of War in the Middle Ages* (revised edition, Ithaca, New York: Cornell University Press, 1953). Individual battles have been described, often by local or amateur historians, over and over again, but much of this work is of limited value. Most of the major engagements are covered in A. H. Burne's *The Battlefields of England* (London: Methuen, 1950) and for Blore Heath see his *More Battlefields of England* (London: Methuen, 1952), but both contain a number of inaccuracies and misconceptions. Among the many papers on particular engagements, it is worth singling out J. D. Blyth, 'The Battle of Tewkesbury', *Transactions of the Bristol and Gloucestershire Archaeological Society*, vol. LXX (1961) and P. W. Hammond (and others), *The Battle of Tewkesbury 4th May 1471* (Tewkesbury Festival Committee, 1971). For Bosworth the most recent account, by D. T. Williams, *The Battle of Bosworth* (Leicester: University Press, 1973), raises a number of difficulties, and there is much of value still to be found in J. Gairdner, 'The Battle of Bosworth', *Archaeologia*, 2nd series, vol. V (1897). For the war in the north-east (1461–64) there are two useful papers by Dorothy Charlesworth, 'The Battle of Hexham' and 'Northumberland in the Early Years of Edward IV', in *Archaeologia Aeliana*, 4th series, vols. XXX and XXXI (1952, 1953).

For the impact of civil war on English politics and society, the material is very diffuse and scattered. The beginnings of the modern reinterpretation are to be found in C. L. Kingsford's pioneering essay, 'Social Life and the Wars of the Roses', in his *Prejudice and Promise in Fifteenth-Century England* (Oxford: Clarendon Press, 1925). A valuable and well-researched regional study is by W. I. Haward, 'Economic Aspects of the Wars of the Roses in East Anglia', *English Historical Review*, vol. XLI (1926); in the same context, see R. L. Storey, 'Lincolnshire and the Wars of the Roses', *Nottingham Medieval Studies*, vol. XIV (1970), and H. T. Evans, *Wales and the Wars of the Roses* (Cambridge: University Press, 1915); and, for the towns, J. E. Winston, *English Towns in the Wars of the Roses* (Princeton: University Press, 1921). Much valuable primary material is to be found in *The Paston Letters*, ed. J. Gairdner (6 vols; London: Chatto and Windus, 1904), of which the first volume forms a long and useful introduction to the interaction of local and national politics. H. S. Bennett, *The Pastons and their England* (Cambridge: University Press, 1922, and later paperback editions), and P. M. Kendall, *The Yorkist Age: Daily Life during the Wars of the Roses* (London: George Allen and Unwin, 1962) are also of interest. J. R. Lander, 'Attainder and Forfeiture, 1453 to 1509', *The Historical Journal*, vol. IV (1961), deals very effectively with a particular aspect of the repercussions of the civil war for the nobility and gentry.

For English civilization during the Wars of the Roses, there is a profusion of material. J. H. Harvey, *Gothic England: A Survey of National Culture, 1300–1550* (London: Batsford, 1947), provides an eloquent appraisal of the splendours of late-medieval English architecture. There is also much material to be found in the relevant volumes of the Pelican History of Art, edited by Nikolaus Pevsner. For castle and country-house building there is a good introduction by R. Allen Brown, *English Castles* (London: Batsford, 1954), but very often the best and most reliable descriptions are to be found in the series of Official Guidebooks to individual buildings published by Her Majesty's Stationery Office on behalf of the Department of the Environment (e.g. Raglan Castle and Tretower Court).

For anyone who wishes to pursue the subject in greater depth, there is now available an excellent, scholarly and up-to-date bibliography by Dr De Lloyd J. Guth, *England 1377–1485* (Cambridge: University Press, 1976).

Some of the books and articles to have appeared since the first printing are: M. A. Hicks, *False, Fleeting, Perjur'd Clarence* (Gloucester: Alan Sutton, 1980); John Gillingham, *The Wars of the Roses: peace and conflict in fifteenth century England* (London: Weidenfeld and Nicholson, 1981); Anthony Goodman, *The Wars of the Roses: military activity and English Society, 1452–1497* (London: Routledge and Kegan Paul, 1981); R. A. Griffiths, *The Reign of Henry VI* (London: Ernest Benn, 1981); Charles Ross, *Richard III* (London: Eyre Methuen, 1981); R. A. Griffiths and R. S. Thomas, *The Making of the Tudor Dynasty* (Gloucester: Alan Sutton, 1985), mainly about Henry Tudor in exile, the build-up to the Bosworth campaign and the campaign and the battle itself; C. F. Richmond, 'The Battle of Bosworth', *History Today*, 25, August 1985, 17–22, which argues that the battle of Bosworth did not take place at its traditional place but at Dadlington nearby and that accepted accounts of the battle – including my own – are wrong.

LIST OF ILLUSTRATIONS

Statuts de l'Ordre de Saint-Michel, attributed to J. Fouquet (*c.* 1420–80); MS fr. 19819 f. 1. *Bibliothèque Nationale, Paris*

74 Acts of mercy of Margaret of York; miniatures by Jean Dreux, MS 9296 f. 1 and f. 17; 15th century. *Bibliothèque Royale, Brussels*

75 Charles the Bold; portrait by Roger van der Weyden (*c.* 1399–1464). *Gemäldegalerie, Berlin.* Photo Jörg P. Anders

Wedding feast; miniature from Jean Wauquelin, *Histoire du Grand Alexandre*; MS Dutuit 456 f. 133; French, *c.* 1454. *Petit Palais, Paris.* Photo Bulloz

76 Edward IV; drawing on first membrane of King's Bench Plea Roll, Hilary Term, 1466; KB 27/819. *Public Record Office, London*

78 Anthony Woodville, Lord Scales and 2nd Earl Rivers, presenting a book to Edward IV and Queen Elizabeth Woodville; miniature from *Dictes and Sayings of Philosophers*; MS 265 f. VI; 15th century. *By permission of His Grace the Archbishop of Canterbury and the Trustees of Lambeth Palace Library*

79 Ann Devereux and her husband William Herbert, Earl of Pembroke, kneeling before Edward IV; miniature from John Lydgate, *Troy Book*; Royal MS 18 D II f. 6; *c.* 1461–62. *British Library*

81 Battle-scene; miniature from *Les Commentaires de César*; Royal MS 16 G VIII f. 189; probably Flemish, 15th century. *British Library*

83 Edward IV receiving book from author; miniature from Jean de Wavrin, *Chronique d'Angleterre*; Royal MS 15 E IV f. 14; Flemish, late 15th century. *British Library*

84 Page from Richard III's prayer book; miniature, MS 474 f. 15r; *c.* 1440. *By permission of His Grace the Archbishop of Canterbury and the Trustees of Lambeth Palace Library*

87 Louis de Gruthuyse; detail of portrait ascribed to 'the Master of the Princely Portraits'; Flemish, 15th century. *Musée Groeninge, Bruges.* Photo A.C.L.

88 The English landing at Lisbon; detail of miniature from Jean de Wavrin, *Chronique d'Angleterre*; Royal MS 14 E IV f. 195; Flemish, late 15th century. *British Library*

91 Edward IV's invasion of France, 1475; miniature from *Mémoires de Ph. de Commines*; MS 18 f. 109; French, early 16th century, Nantes. Photo Giraudon

92 Lady Margaret Beaufort; anonymous painter, mid-16th century. *Courtesy of the Master and Fellows of St John's College, Cambridge*

95 Richard III, his queen, Anne Nevill, and their son Edward; drawing from the *Rous Roll*; Add. MS 48976; English, 15th century. *British Library*

96 Edward V; panel, English, 16th century; St George's Chapel, Windsor

99 Henry VII, portrait drawing from the *Recueil d'Arras*, attributed to Jacques Leboucq; 16th century. Photo Giraudon

Margaret Beaufort, Countess of Richmond; bronze effigy by Pietro Torrigiano, 1512–18; Westminster Abbey. *Copyright Warburg Institute.* Photo Helmut Gernsheim

Elizabeth of York, Henry VII's queen; bronze effigy by Pietro Torrigiano, 1512–18; Westminster Abbey. *Copyright Warburg Institute.* Photo Helmut Gernsheim

100 John Howard, Duke of Norfolk; copy of stained-glass window, now destroyed, in Tendring Hall, Suffolk

102–3 Royal combat; miniature from Jean Wauquelin, *Histoire du Grand Alexandre*; MS Dutuit 456 f. 33; French, *c.* 1454. *Petit Palais, Paris.* Photo Bulloz

105 John de la Pole, Earl of Lincoln (d. 1487), and his wife, sister of Edward IV; alabaster effigies, Wingfield Church, Suffolk. Photo Canon Ridgway

106 Elizabeth of York; anonymous master, late 16th century. *National Portrait Gallery, London*

107 Henry VII; portrait by Michael Sittow, 1505. *National Portrait Gallery, London*

108 Battle of Barnet, 1471; miniature from the French version of the *Historie of the Arrivall of Edward IV*; MS 236; late 15th century. *University of Ghent*

110 Battle of Crécy, 1346; miniature from *Chroniques de Froissart*; French, late 15th century. *Bibliothèque Nationale, Paris*

168 Entrance tower, Ightham Mote, Kent; 1480. Photo Kerry Dundas

Hurstmonceux Castle, Sussex; second quarter of 15th century

169 Raglan Castle, Wales, completed in the 1460s. Photo Department of the Environment

Tretower Court, Brecon; late 15th century. Photo National Monuments Record

171 Tretower Court, Brecon; late 15th century. Photo National Monuments Record

172 Kirby Muxloe, Leicestershire, 1480–83. Photo Christina Gascoigne

173 Church tower of Huish Episcopi, Somerset; late 15th century. Photo Edwin Smith

174 Blacksmith; woodcut from William Caxton's *Game and Play of the Chess*, 1483. *British Library*

175 The Squire; woodcut from Chaucer's *Canterbury Tales*, printed by Wynkyn de Worde, 1498. *British Library*

176 Game of chess; woodcut from Caxton's edition of Jacobus de Cesolis, *Game of Chess*, c. 1482. *British Library*

177 Fan-vault of Sherborne Abbey, Dorset; last quarter of 15th century. Photo Edwin Smith

INDEX

Page numbers in italics refer to illustrations. Kings, queens and princes have been indexed by their Christian names, noblemen by their titles, and bishops by their sees. Many place-names referred to only incidentally have been omitted.